EDITOR: LEE JOHNSO

OSPREY MILITARY

ELITE SERIES 6J

GERMAN MOUNTAIN & SKI TROOPS 1939-45

Text by
GORDON WILLIAMSON
Colour plates by
STEPHEN ANDREW

First published in Great Britain in 1996 by
Osprey Publishing, Elms Court, Chapel Way, Botley,
Oxford OX2 9LP, United Kingdom.
Email: *osprey@osprey-publishing.co.uk*

ISBN 1 85532 572 1

Filmset in Great Britain by KDI, Newton le Willows
Printed through World Print Ltd, Hong Kong

FOR A CATALOGUE OF ALL BOOKS PUBLISHED BY
OSPREY MILITARY, AUTOMOTIVE AND AVIATION
PLEASE WRITE TO:

The Marketing Manager, Osprey Publishing,
PO Box 140, Wellingborough, Northants, NN8 4ZA,
United Kingdom

VISIT OSPREY'S WEBSITE AT:

http://www.osprey-publishing.co.uk

Publishers' note

Readers may wish to study this title in conjunction with the
following Osprey publications:

Elite	34	*Afrikakorps*
MAA	24	*The Panzer Divisions*
MAA	34	*The Waffen-SS*
MAA	124	*German Commanders of WW2*
MAA	213	*German MP Units*
MAA	139	*German Airborne Troops*
MAA	282	*Axis Forces in Yugoslavia*

Artist's note

Readers may care to note that the original paintings from
which the colour plates in this book were prepared are available for private sale. All reproduction copyright whatsoever is
retained by the Publishers. All enquiries should be addressed
to:

Stephen Andrew
87 Ellisland
Kirkintilloch
Glasgow
G66 2UA

The Publishers regret that they can enter into no correspon-
dence upon this matter.

INTRODUCTION

Although reference to the elite units of the German armed forces in the Second World War usually brings to mind troops such as the Fallschirmjäger, the Panzertruppe or the Waffen-SS, there is one much neglected branch of the front line fighting forces which deserves the accolade 'elite' as much as any other: the mountain infantry of the Gebirgstruppe.

*An Unteroffizier of Gebirgstruppe during a climbing exercise. Note the **Bergmütze** and M36-pattern field blouse. He wears the mountain-boots and puttees. (Josef Charita)*

To the Germans, the Gebirgsjäger, or mountain infantryman, was a relatively new member of the fighting forces, dating back only as far as 1915, when the first mountain troop units were formed in Bavaria. They comprised battle-hardened soldiers from the states of Bavaria and Württemberg. They acquitted themselves superbly well in battle, under officers of the calibre of the young Erwin Rommel (he won his *Pour-le-Merite* while commanding a mountain troops unit).

After the end of the First World War a hard core of experienced mountain troop personnel was retained by the army of the Weimar Republic, so that when Hitler repudiated the Treaty of Versailles, in 1935, and set about rebuilding the German Army, the nucleus of the first new Gebirgs division was already to hand.

The *Anschluss* with Austria, in 1938, saw many trained and experienced mountain troops from the Austrian Army, which had a much longer history in mountain warfare than Germany, flow into the Wehrmacht. Indeed, their numbers were sufficient to constitute two new Gebirgs divisions.

Gebirgsjäger were basically light infantry, trained for mountain warfare. The type of terrain in which they operated dictated that the support elements available to traditional infantry divisions, such as heavy artillery, armoured vehicles, and even tanks, could not be used by the Gebirgsjäger. Apart from some lighter calibre artillery and howitzers, usually of a type which could be disassembled and carried by pack mules, the Gebirgsjäger fought principally as infantry assault formations, and it was in this role they excelled.

The typical Gebirgsjäger was a supremely fit individual. Not only was he often obliged to carry a considerable amount of personal kit around with him in his rucksack (kit which the divisional baggage train would usually carry for the traditional infantryman), but he was also expected to scale mountains while doing so

Gebirgsjäger Major Karl Eisgruber. Note the metal Edelweiss insignia of the left side flap of the cap and the typical two-button fastening. The Waffenfarbe colour strips to the centre of each bar of the collar patch are in light green. (Josef Charita)

Later in the war, these superbly trained troops often found themselves, like their Fallschirmjäger contemporaries, thrown into the line as ordinary infantry, far from their beloved mountain environment, and they frequently suffered as a result.

Morale and *esprit de corps* in mountain troop units was almost universally very high, and commanders such as Eduard Dietl, the 'Hero of Narvik', or Julius 'Papa' Ringel were idolised by their men. When in their element – the high mountain peaks of Norway or the Caucasus – the Gebirgsjäger fought with an *élan* and determination which were second to none.

It is interesting to note that the first soldier of the Wehrmacht to be awarded the coveted

Oakleaves to the Knights Cross of the Iron Cross was a Gebirgsjäger, Generaloberst Eduard Dietl, whose name was adopted by the training school of the Gebirgsjäger of the present day German Bundeswehr, the 'Dietl Kaserne'.

MOUNTAIN DIVISIONS

1.Gebirgs-Division

Commanders
Generalmajor Ludwig Kubler (1937-41)
Generalmajor Hubert Lanz (1942-43)
Generalmajor Hermann Kress (1943)
Generalleutnant Walter Stettner,
Ritter von Graberhofen (1943-44)
Generalleutnant Josef Kubler (1945)

Main Constituent Units
Gebirgsjäger Regiment 98
Gebirgsjäger Regiment 99
Gebirgs-Artillerie Regiment 79
Panzerjäger Abteilung 54
Gebirgs-Pionier Abteilung 54
Gebirgs-Nachrichten Abteilung 54

This division was formed in April 1938, and was based in Garmisch, Bavaria; its parent *Wehrkreis*, or military district, was Wehrkreis VII. After the *Anschluss* with Austria, in 1938, a number of Austrian personnel were also taken on in strength. The division had originally featured a third Gebirgsjäger Regiment, the 100th, which was transferred to 5.Gebirgs Division in 1940. As part of XIV Armee, it took part in the invasion of Poland, capturing the Dukla Pass in the Carpathian mountains. It also performed with distinction during the attack on France and the Low Countries in 1940, at the crossings of the Maas and Loire rivers, and took part in the invasion of Yugoslavia.

In the summer of 1941, 1.Gebirgs Division was part of Hitler's invasion force which poured over the borders of the Soviet Union. It was attached to Heeresgruppe Sud and saw action at the Uman Pocket, Kiev, Stalino and at the crossing of the Dnieper.

In the spring of 1942, 1.Gebirgs Division fought as part of 1.Panzerarmee in the Donets area. That summer it spearheaded the drive into the Caucasus and remained in that area until 1943. It took part in the defensive battles in southern Russia after the debacle at Stalingrad, until March 1943, when it was withdrawn into Greece. There it was held as part of the Oberkommando der Wehrmacht's strategic reserve, spending its time engaged in anti-partisan duties until April 1944, when it was despatched to Hungary. It was briefly withdrawn from the front in August, but returned to Hungary in the December as part of 2.Panzerarmee for the last great German offensive in the east, around Lake Balaton (the Platensee).

A combined forces group during the battle for Narvik, comprising Kriegsmarine, Luftwaffe and Gebirgsjäger personnel.

Towards the end of the war it was renamed 1.Volks-Gebirgs-Division; and it found itself fighting in the south-eastern part of Austria when the war ended. Its personnel went into Soviet captivity, and many never returned.

2.Gebirgs-Division

Commanders
Generalleutnant Valentin Feuerstein (1938-41)
Generalmajor Ernst Schlemmer (1941-42)
Generalleutnant Ritter Georg von Hengl (1942-43)
Generalmajor Hans Degan (1944-45)

Main Constituent Units
Gebirgs-Infanterie Regiment 136
Gebirgs-Infanterie Regiment 137
Gebirgs-Artillerie Regiment 111
Radfahrer Abteilung 67
Gebirgs-Panzerjäger Abteilung 47

A mixed group of Gebirgsjäger and Kriegsmarine sailors from the sunk German destroyer flotilla in the hills above Narvik in 1940.

A German sailor, his vessel sunk or beached, has joined the fight alongside his Gebirgsjäger colleagues, and is seen here reporting to General Dietl.

Gebirgs-Pionier Abteilung 82
Gebirgs-Nachrichten Abteilung 67

The 2.Gebirgs Division home-base was in Innsbruck, Austria, Wehrkreis XVIII. This was one of the divisions formed primarily from Tyrolean Austrians after the *Anschluss*. When war broke out the division served as part of Heeresgruppe Sud in the Polish campaign. It subsequently took part in the invasion of Norway, fighting in the Narvik area in support of 3.Gebirgs Division, which was under considerable pressure from British units. It then spent some time on occupation duties in the far north of Norway and in Lapland.

On the opening of Operation Barbarossa, in June 1941, the division became part of XIX Gebirgskorps in 20.Gebirgsarmee and took part in the drive towards Murmansk. It served in this corps in the same theatre until late 1944, when the Finns concluded their own peace agreement with the Soviet Union, and the German units in Lapland withdrew into Norway. The division suffered badly during the Russian winter offensive of 1944-45.

A transfer to the Western Front followed, and the main combat regiments were rebuilt and reinforced, though the quality of the replacements did not match that of the division's original complement. It joined Heeresgruppe G at the front in February 1945 and took part in the fighting for the Saar and Moselle areas before retreating into southern Germany where it joined XII Korps. Their battered remnants surrendered to the Americans in May 1945.

3.Gebirgs-Division

Commanders
Generalleutnant Eduard Dietl (1938-40)
Generalleutnant Hans Kreysing (1940-43)

General Dietl, watched by two Kriegsmarine officers, is about to take to his skis on the hill above Narvik. Note the puttees and mountain-boots. The wide red generals' stripes can just be seen on his breeches on the original print. His tunic is a generals' version of the M36-style field blouse.

Generalleutnant August Wittmann (1943-44)
Generalleutnant Paul Klatt (1945)

Main Constituent Units
Gebirgs-Infanterie Regiment 138
Gebirgs-Infanterie Regiment 139
Gebirgs-Artillerie Regiment 112
Radfahr Abteilung 68
Gebirgs-Panzerjäger Abteilung 48
Gebirgs-Pionier Abteilung 83
Gebirgs-Nachrichten Abteilung 68

This division was formed by the amalgamation of the former Austrian 5. and 7.Gebirgs divisions after the *Anschluss*. On the outbreak of hostilities in 1939, the division was part of XVIII Korps of 14 Armee, one of the constituent units of Heeresgruppe Sud, and took part in the successful Polish campaign. Thereafter it was transferred to the Western Front, and in March was withdrawn from the front to prepare for its part in the forth-coming campaign in Norway.

It was chosen as the spearhead unit of the invasion force at Narvik in April 1940. One of the division's regiments, the 138th, was detached to capture Trondheim, leaving the force which took Narvik seriously weakened, and when the British expeditionary force arrived at the port, the division found itself in the midst of some very bitter fighting. It was a close run thing, and Dietl admitted that he had considered withdrawing his battered troops over the border into Swedish internment. However, the division fought on determinedly, and finally won the day, but only after over two months of heavy fighting.

The 3.Gebirgs Division subsequently took part in the opening stages of the invasion of the Soviet Union, during the drive from northern Finland towards the port of Murmansk. It remained in this sector until autumn 1942, when it was moved to the southern sector of the front, which was coming under severe pressure from Soviet counter-attacks. It took part in the attempt to relieve 6.Armee at Stalingrad.

The division then fought in the defensive battles in the Ukraine, before withdrawing through Hungary into Czechoslovakia, where it became part of XXXXIX Panzerkorps. It was in action in

After the successful conclusion of the Narvik battle, General Dietl relaxes with some fellow officers aboard a Norwegian fishing boat. The heavily studded soles of his mountain-boots are clearly visible.

Upper Silesia when the war ended, and it surrendered to Soviet forces.

4.Gebirgs-Division

Commanders
Generalleutnant Karl Eglseer (1940-42)
Generalleutnant Hermann Kress (1943)
Generalleutnant Julius Braun (1944)
Generalleutnant Friedrich Breith (1944-45)

Main Constituent Units
Gebirgs-Infanterie Regiment 13
Gebirgs-Infanterie Regiment 91
Gebirgs-Artillerie Regiment 94
Radfahr Abteilung 94

tles at Uman, where it suffered heavy casualties.

In the German summer offensive of 1942 the division struck into the Caucasus mountains and fought with some distinction, becoming involved in the containment of the attempted Russian landings at Novorossisk in the Kuban bridgehead. In 1944, having taken part in the ferocious battles around the Dnieper Bend, it received a commendation from Generalfeldmarschall von Manstein for the part it had played in the destruction of the Soviet 1st Tank Army.

In late 1944 the division withdrew across the Carpathian mountains into Hungary, and was involved in the fighting retreat into Czechoslovakia and Austria, ending up as part of 1.Panzerarmee. By the end of the war this once powerful division had been reduced to a Kampfgruppe; it surrendered on 9 May 1945.

A troop of Gebirgsjäger heading into the mountains with their heavily laden pack mules. The Gebirgsjäger are all wearing greatcoats and carrying the large issue rucksacks. (Ian Jewison)

Gebirgs-Panzerjäger Abteilung 94
Gebirgs-Pionier Abteilung 94
Gebirgs-Nachrichten Abteilung 94

This division was newly formed in 1940; its home area was Wehrkreis IV, which covered Saxony and parts of Prussia and Silesia. It comprised mostly German, rather than Austrian, personnel, with drafts from other units including 25. and 27.Infanterie Divisions.

The division was in training until the spring of 1941, when it became part of 12.Armee for the attack on Yugoslavia. After the successful conclusion of the Balkan campaign it then became part of 17.Armee in Heeresgruppe Sud for the invasion of the Soviet Union. Taking part in the advance towards the Volga, it fought in the bat-

*The **Bergmütze** can be seen to particularly good effect on this shot. Note the typical high crown and short peak. The officer shown here is wearing the issue raincoat. (Josef Charita)*

5.Gebirgs-Division

Commanders
Generalleutnant Julius Ringel (1940-44)
Generalmajor Max-Gunther Schrank (1945)

Main Constituent Units
Gebirgs-Infanterie Regiment 85
Gebirgs-Infanterie Regiment 100
Gebirgs-Artillerie Regiment 95
Radfahr Abteilung 95
Gebirgs-Panzerjäger Abteilung 95
Gebirgs-Pionier Abteilung 95
Gebirgs-Nachrichten Abteilung 95

This elite division was formed in autumn 1940 and for most of its life was commanded by the popular and charismatic Julius 'Papa' Ringel. Although its home base was in Salzburg, Austria, 5.Gebirgs Division personnel were predominantly Bavarian.

Its first few months were spent training in the Bavarian Alps; it then moved to the Balkans theatre, where it played a prominent part in the smashing of the Metaxas defence lines and the subsequent defeat of the Greek and Commonwealth forces.

Within weeks of the successful conclusion of the campaign in Greece, Ringel's Gebirgsjäger were to become part of the German assault force launched against the island of Crete. During the Battle of Maleme, these tough mountain troops came to the aid of the beleaguered Fallschirmjäger in what was to become the turning point of the operation on Crete.

From late summer 1941 to March 1942 the division was allowed a period of rest and refitting. However, it soon returned to battle, this time on the Eastern Front, where it was attached to Heeresgruppe Nord, serving in the Volkhov region on the Leningrad front. It remained in this sector until the end of 1943, distinguishing itself on a number of occasions.

In December 1943 the division was transferred to Italy under the control of 10.Armee. It took part in the fighting retreat up the 'leg' of the Italian mainland, distinguishing itself yet again during the battles for the Gustav and Gothic

General Eduard Dietl after the Battle of Narvik. Note the Narvik Shield worn on the left sleeve of his pre-war pattern General's service tunic. The Knights Cross with Oakleaves is also being worn. (Josef Charita)

defence lines. Towards the end of the war, it was fighting in the border region between Italy and France, and eventually surrendered to American forces in April 1945.

6.Gebirgs-Division

Commanders
Generalmajor Ferdinand Schörner (1940-42)
Generalleutnant Philipp Christian (1942-44)
Generalmajor Max Pemsel (1944-45)

Main Constituent Units
Gebirgs-Infanterie Regiment 141
Gebirgs-Infanterie Regiment 143
Gebirgs-Artillerie Regiment 118
Gebirgs-Kraftrad Abteilung 157

A Gebirgsjäger MG42 machine-gun team on the Eastern Front. Although the soldier to the left wears a lightweight summer issue tunic, the Obergefreiter with binoculars wears a heavy wool greatcoat. The latter is a veteran of the battle for Narvik. (Josef Charita)

Gebirgs-Panzerjäger Abteilung 157
Gebirgs-Pionier Abteilung 91
Gebirgs-Nachrichten Abteilung 96

Formed in 1940, this division began its war in occupation duties in France, before being transferred to 12.Armee in Poland. When the Balkan campaign began, the division moved south, taking part in the brief campaign against Greece and in particular in the smashing of the Metaxas line. Although some elements may have taken part in the Crete operation, the bulk of the division stayed on in Greece as part of the occupation force, before being moved to Norway in September 1941.

As part of Gebirgskorps Norwegen, it took part in the drive into Russia, towards the port of Murmansk. It remained in the far northern sector of the Russian front until late 1944, when the

Finns reached a separate surrender agreement with the Soviets. At this point it withdrew back into Norway, where it surrendered to the British at the end of the war.

7.Gebirgs-Division

Commander
Generalleutnant August Krakau

Main Constituent Units
Gebirgs-Infanterie Regiment 144
Gebirgs-Infanterie Regiment 206
Gebirgs-Artillerie Regiment 82
Kraftrad Abteilung 99
Gebirgs-Panzerjäger Abteilung 99
Gebirgs-Pionier Abteilung 99
Gebirgs-Nachrichten Abteilung 99

This formation was originally intended as a Jäger unit: it was formed in 1940 as 99.Jäger Division, and served as such on the southern sector of the Eastern Front. In the winter of 1941/42 it was withdrawn from the front and returned to

A fine portrait study of Oberst Wolf Hagemann, who was awarded the Knights Cross of the Iron Cross on 4 September 1940 as a major in command of III Batallion, Gebirgsjäger-Regiment 139. He later won the Oakleaves, on 4 June 1944, while on the Eastern Front. The Gebirgsjäger arm patch and Narvik shield are clearly visible. (Josef Charita)

This photo shows Generalleutnant Kubler making the award of the Knights Cross of the Iron Cross to Unteroffizier Georg Audenrieth. The Gebirgsjäger arm patch on Audenrieth's sleeve is clearly visible. (Josef Charita)

Germany, where it was re-formed as a Gebirgs division. In early 1942, as 7.Gebirgs Division, it returned to action, rejoining the front in Finland.

This division remained in this sector until the Finns concluded their peace negotiations with the Soviets, at which point it withdrew through Lapland into Norway and became part of XVIII Gebirgskorps. In 1945 it was supposed to be returning to Germany to aid in the defensive battles there, but the war ended before the transfer could be made. The division surrendered to the British in Norway.

8.Gebirgs-Division

Not a great deal is known about this particular unit. It was formed in 1942 in Norway and is believed to have comprised 142. and 144.Gebirgs-Infanterie Regiments and Gebirgs-Artillerie Regiment 124, presumably with the usual

Part of a Gebirgsjäger regiment moves through the snows of a Russian mountain pass. Note that all wear the **Bergmütze** *and carry heavily laden rucksacks. To the rear of the column are some of the unit's pack mules carrying heavy equipment. (Ian Jewison)*

Panzerjäger, Pionier and Nachrichten support units. It is not believed to have reached full strength, but saw action in the far north of the Eastern Front until late 1944, when it was transferred to Italy and saw action in the Po Valley area. At this time it numbered only around 3,000 men, and was on the Order of Battle of 10.Armee. It surrendered in Italy in April 1945.

9.Gebirgs-Division

The confused situation in the closing stages of the war led to two divisions being allocated this same number. The first 9.Gebirgs-Division was in fact only of Kampfgruppe strength, and was commanded by Generalmajor Krautler. It was formed in Norway from troops who had taken part in the retreat through Finland, and surrendered to the British in 1945. The second unit was also merely a small battle group, Kampfgruppe Semmering, formed to defend the Semmering Pass in Austria from the advancing Soviets. An *ad hoc* unit, it included personnel from the Gebirgs-Artillerie Schule in Dachstein, the SS-Gebirgs-Ersatz Batallion-Leoben and even redundant Luftwaffe personnel from Jagdgeschwader Boelke. Officially

Oberfeldwebel Rudolf Schlee, a platoon leader in 6.Kompanie, Gebirgsjäger-Regiment 13. Having won the Knights Cross of the Iron Cross in October 1941, Schlee went on to win the coveted Oakleaves on 6 April 1943. Note the infantry assault badge, the combat award most commonly won by Gebirgsjäger. His metal Edelweiss badge has been backed with dark green cloth, a popular fashion in some units. (Josef Charita)

it formed part of III Panzerkorps, in 6.Armee. By the end of the war, the unit had become fragmented; some managed to escape westwards into the American zone; others were less fortunate and went into Soviet captivity.

188.Gebirgs-Division

This unit originated as a reserve division used principally for training Gebirgsjäger, who would then be posted on to one of the other Gebirgs divisions. In the latter part of 1944 it was redesignated to the status of a full Gebirgs-Division and saw limited service in the Balkans before being swallowed up in the collapse of the Eastern Front in 1945. Its commander was Generalleutnant Wilhelm von Hosslin.

1.Ski-Jäger-Division

This unit was created in late 1943. It was initially a brigade, but was expanded to become a division in Bavaria in mid-1944. Its principal units were Ski-Jäger Regiments 1. and 2., together with the usual Pionier, Nachrichten and Panzerjäger elements. The division was first committed to battle in the central sector of the Eastern Front in the summer of 1944, and took part in the fighting retreat towards the Vistula. Later in the year it was moved to Czechoslovakia, but went north into Poland before the end of the year. By the end of the war it was back in Czechoslovakia, where it surrendered to the Russians in May 1945.

The division was commanded by Generalleutnant Gustav Hundt (1944-45).

Apparently the Germans did not consider that the division had been particularly successful, as no attempt was made to create a second Ski-Jäger division. However, ten of the division's personnel performed with sufficient distinction to receive the Knights Cross of the Iron Cross.

Mention should also be made of the Hochgebirgsjäger battalions. Four were formed, and it was intended that they would operate in the very highest mountain peaks. However, it was subsequently decided that there was no real need for such highly specialised units within the Gebirgsjäger arm, and the personnel were distributed to the mainstream Gebirgs divisions. Before their disbandment, however, Battalions 1 and 2

Oberfeldwebel Adam Ebner, a Knights Cross winner from 3. Kompanie, Gebirgsjäger-Regiment 137. A veteran of Narvik, he is also a qualified paratrooper, evident from the **Fallschirmschutzenabzeichen** *on his left breast pocket. (Josef Charita)*

saw action on the Eastern Front, while 3 and 4 saw action in Italy. Hochgebirgsjäger-Batallion 3 performed exceptionally well, seeing service at Monte Cassino, and one of its soldiers received the Knights Cross of the Iron Cross for gallantry.

WAFFEN-SS UNITS

6.SS-Gebirgs-Division 'Nord'

Commanders
SS-Brigadeführer Richard Herrmann (1940-41)
SS-Brigadeführer Karl Demelhuber (1941-42)

Gebirgsjäger trudging through the heavy snow on the Eastern Front in the winter of 1942/43. All are wearing the greatcoat and are armed with the basic weapon of the German infantry, the Mauser Kar98k carbine. (Josef Charita)

SS-Gruppenführer Matthias Kleinheisterkamp
(1942–43)
SS-Gruppenführer Lothar Debes
(1944)
SS-Obergruppenführer Friedrich-Wilhelm Kruger (1944)
SS-Gruppenführer Karl-Heinrich Brenner
(1944–45)

Main Constituent Units

SS-Gebirgsjäger-Regiment 11
'Reinhard Heydrich'
SS-Gebirgsjäger-Regiment 12
'Michael Gaissmair'
SS-Gebirgs-Artillerie Regiment 6
SS-Gebirgs-Nachrichtenabteilung 6
SS-Panzerjäger Abteilung 6
SS-Gebirgs-Aufklärungsabteilung 6

SS-Flak Abteilung 6
SS-Gebirgs-Pionierabteilung 6

First created as Kampfgruppe 'Nord' in early 1941 from Totenkopfstandarten 6 and 7, to which were added the Nachrichtenabteilung from the SS-Verfügungsdivision, the unit first saw action in the far north sector of the Eastern Front, and took part in the unsuccessful drive towards Murmansk.

The Kampfgruppe was upgraded to divisional status in late 1941, and was recruited from a mixture of both German (Reichsdeutsche) and ethnic German (Volksdeutsche) personnel.

It did not fare particularly well in its early period on the Eastern Front. The terrain was

Friedrich Hengstler, shown here as a lieutenant, won the Knights Cross of the Iron Cross as an Oberfeldwebel in Gebirgsjäger Regiment 98. Of particular interest is the Heeresbergführer badge on the left breast pocket. (Josef Charita)

dark, damp swampland and forests and the unit suffered heavy casualties at the hands of the Soviets. Some of its soldiers are said to have fled in panic during one Soviet attack and that the situation was only saved by Wehrmacht and Finnish units on its flanks.

Nevertheless it remained on this sector of the front until September 1944, and while it was there was re-formed as a Gebirgs-Division. As part of XVIII Gebirgskorps, it took part in the retreat through Lapland into Norway, forming part of the corps' rearguard.

In late 1944 it was withdrawn from Norway and shipped to Denmark, whence it joined the German forces on the Western Front. Fragmented during the transfer, the first units to arrive were formed into a battle group, SS-Kampfgruppe 'Nord', which took part in the closing stages of the Ardennes offensive. Joined by the remainder of the division, it fought in the retreat through the Saarland and acquitted itself much better here than it had on the Eastern Front. It put up a pugnacious defence against powerful American attacks, but was finally fragmented by overwhelming Allied superiority in numbers.

Scattered elements from the division attached themselves to other SS units and continued to fight to the bitter end. The last remaining divisional elements surrendered to the US army in Bavaria at the end of the war.

The charismatic and highly popular General der Gebirgstruppe Julius 'Papa' Ringel, commander of 5.Gebirgs-Division.

7.SS-Freiwilligen-Gebirgs-Division 'Prinz Eugen'

Commanders

SS-Gruppenführer Artur Phleps (1942-43)
SS-Brigadeführer Reichsritter Carl von Oberkamp (1944)
SS-Brigadeführer Otto Kumm (1944-45)
SS-Oberführer August Schmidhuber (1945)

Main Constituent Units

SS-Gebirgsjäger Regiment 13 'Artur Phleps'
SS-Gebirgsjäger Regiment 14
SS-Gebirgs-Artillerie Regiment 7
SS-Gebirgs-Aufklärungsabteilung 7
SS-Panzerjager Abteilung 7
SS-Gebirgs-Pionier Abteilung 7

SS-Gebirgs-Nachrichten Abteilung 7
SS-Flak Abteilung 7

In 1942 the order was given for the formation of a new Volksdeutsche volunteer division, to be officered by those who had served in the Hapsburg army. In April 1942 the new division, entitled SS-Freiwilligen-Division 'Prinz Eugen', was experiencing considerable difficulty getting its uniforms, equipment and armaments. In fact, throughout its life the division had, to some extent, to depend on captured equipment.

Under the command of Artur Phleps, a former general in the Romanian army, the division went into action in October 1942 against Tito's partisans in Serbia. It subsequently took part in anti-partisan actions throughout Montenegro,

*A fine portrait study of Knights Cross holder Leutnant Michael Pössinger of Gebirgsjäger Regiment 98. Shown here wearing the Knights Cross, Pössinger was also to win the Oakleaves, in February 1945. The Gebirgsjäger arm patch is clearly shown, as is the T-shaped backing to the insignia on his **Bergmütze**. (Pössinger)*

Bosnia and Herzogovina, and was also involved in the disarming of Italian units after Italy's surrender in the summer of 1943. In the spring of 1944 it took part in the attack on Tito's headquarters in Drvar, where SS paratroops were also used in force for the first time: 'Prinz Eugen' smashed Tito's 1st Partisan Division during this battle. As the war progressed, however, the greater danger was to come from advancing Soviet forces. The division covered the retreat of Heeresgruppe E through Yugoslavia, before withdrawing itself, suffering heavy casualties in the process.

The division was reinforced towards the end of the war, and in January 1945 again went on to the offensive against Tito's partisans, achieving considerable success but again suffering heavy casualties.

As part of XXXIV Korps, Heeresgruppe F, the division took part in the retreat northwards, but it was unable to escape as a cohesive unit. Some elements of the division released from their oath of allegiance in the closing moments of the war, managed to escape westwards, but most were forced to surrender to Tito's partisans. Very few of those who went into captivity survived.

13.Waffen-Gebirgs-Division Der SS 'Handschar' (Kroatische Nr. 1)

Commanders
SS-Oberführer von Obwurzer (1943)
SS-Brigadeführer Sauberzweig (1943-44)
SS-Brigadeführer Desiderius Hampel (1944-45)

Main Constituent Units
Waffen-Gebirgsjäger Regiment der SS 27
Waffen-Gebirgsjäger Regiment der SS 28
Waffen-Gebirgs-Artillerie Regiment der SS 13
SS-Aufklärungs Abteilung (mot) 13
Waffen-Gebirgs Pionier Abteilung der SS 13
Waffen-Gebirgs Nachrichten Abteilung der SS 13
Waffen-Panzerjäger Abteilung der SS 13
Waffen-Flak Abteilung der SS 13

*A group of Gebirgsjäger relax during a lull in the fighting on the northern sector of the Eastern Front. Note the **Bergmütze**, with its Edelweiss badge, balanced on the knee of the soldier in the foreground.*

This division was raised in early 1943. It was intended that it be recruited solely from Bosnian Moslem volunteers, but because of a shortage of volunteers, members of the local Christian communities were apparently pressed into service. The division was officered by experienced German Waffen-SS personnel.

Due to considerable opposition to the raising of this division by the pro-German Croat Ustaschi movement, it was to be formed not in its homeland, but far to the west, in occupied France. It went through numerous name-changes during its formation, including Kroatische SS-Freiwilligen Division, Muselmanen Division and SS-Freiwilligen Bosn.-Herzogov.-Gebirgs-Division (Kroatien), before reaching its final designation.

Himmler was keen to retain the goodwill of the

Major Herbert Goriany from Gebirgs-Artillerie Regiment 85. Note the Heeresbergführer badge on the left breast pocket and the standard officers' belt with double claw buckle. (Josef Charita)

Bosnian Moslems, and in a letter to the commander of the 'Prinz Eugen' Division, which was to assist in the formation of 'Handschar', he explained that the volunteers would have, as had their predecessors who had served in the Hapsburg army, full freedom to practise their religion and to wear the traditional fez head-dress.

The division experienced problems almost immediately during its working up period in France. Many of the German personnel training the Moslem recruits had a less than sympathetic attitude towards their charges. Animosity grew to such an extent that some elements of the division mutinied. Retribution was swift: the mutiny was quickly put down and its ringleaders executed. Himmler was furious, however, that the situation had been allowed to deteriorate to such a degree.

With its reliability now uncertain for many Germans, the division was sent into action in January 1944, and it served on anti-partisan duties in northern Bosnia until the autumn of that year. The approach of the Red Army in the latter part of 1944 saw many of the division's Moslem personnel demobilised and simply sent home. The remnants, principally the German cadre personnel,

*Gebirgsjäger from a Gebirgs-Division on the Eastern Front. Unusually, one wears the steel helmet, but his **Bergmütze** can be seen tucked into his waistbelt. The studs and cleats on the soles of the mountain-boots are visible on the soldiers in the foreground. (Ian Jewison)*

fought on as battle groups before being reunited towards the end of the year.

Despite its earlier reputation for lack of reliability, those now remaining in the division fought well, and in the closing stages of the war, five of the division's German cadre personnel were awarded the Knights Cross of the Iron Cross for gallantry and distinguished service. The division saw action in the final German offensive in the area around the Platensee, before being driven westwards into Austria. There they surrendered to British forces at the end of the war.

SS-Sturmbannführer Léon Degrelle, commander of SS-Sturmbrigade 'Wallonie', wears an M43 field-cap with, unusually, an army- rather than SS-pattern Edelweiss, and with the direction of the badge reversed – the stem of the Edelweiss should point towards the front of the cap. This unit was entitled to wear the mountain troop insignia in commemoration of an attachment to a mountain troop unit of the army before the Walloon volunteers were transformed to the Waffen-SS. (Josef Charita)

21.Waffen-Gebirgs-Division Der SS 'Skanderbeg' (Albanische Nr. 1)

Commanders
SS-Standartenführer August Schmidhuber (1944-45)
SS-Obersturmbannführer Graaf (1945)

Main Constituent Units
Waffen-Gebirgsjäger Regiment der SS 50
Waffen-Gebirgsjäger Regiment der SS 51

The other units of the division would have carried the divisional number 21, but the division never reached full strength and it is not known how many of the remaining divisional elements were ever effectively formed.

Raised in 1944, this formation was to have comprised Albanian Moslem volunteers. It suffered from a poor standard of volunteer, many of

Oberstleutnant Richard Ernst, commander of Gebirgsjäger Regiment 100. Note the ribbon of the Blood Order on the right breast pocket flap, indicating that he took part in the abortive Munich Putsch, in November 1923. (Josef Charita)

Bosnian Moslems from the 'Handschar' division relax over a meal in the summer sunshine. Note the tents assembled from camouflaged Zeltbahn buttoned together. (Josef Charita)

A group of Bosnian Moslem volunteers from 13.Waffen-Gebirgs-Division der SS 'Handschar'. Note the fez and the divisional insignia on the collar patch. (Josef Charita)

whom, even at this late stage of the war when every man was needed, were rejected as unsuitable. By the end of the year only around 6,000 or so suitable volunteers had come forward. Lack of appropriate armaments and other equipment also delayed its formation.

Despite not being fully organised, elements of the division were committed to battle against partisan units, with results that were less than impressive. A draft of around 3,000 German personnel, mostly former Kriegsmarine sailors who were now surplus to the requirements of the navy, reached the division in late 1944. With a much greater proportion of dependable German cadre personnel, the division took part in the fighting retreat through the Balkans. The Albanian

A parade of volunteers from the 'Handschar' division. Their collar tabs are visible, but they are not wearing the Edelweiss sleeve patch. Mountain-boots with puttees or gaiters are worn. The fez worn is the burgundy red parade version. (Josef Charita)

Moslem contingent was now deserting at a tremendous rate, with over 3,500 of them fleeing before the war ended. It seemed pointless to retain the remaining Albanians, and they were demobilised. This so-called 'Albanian Volunteer Mountain Division' was in fact now manned predominantly by German sailors.

Retaining the division as an independent unit was no longer feasible, and the German cadre personnel were, in the main, posted to the 'Prinz Eugen' Division. Despite the division's poor record and its short lifespan, a full range of insignia was initiated, including collar patches, armshields and cuff bands.

23.Waffen-Gebirgs-Division der SS 'Kama' (Kroatische Nr. 2)

Commanders
SS-Standartenführer Hellmut Raithel

Main Constituent Units
Waffen-Gebirgsjäger Regiment der SS 55
Waffen-Gebirgsjäger Regiment der SS 56

This particular unit was raised in mid-1944. The officers were mostly Reichsdeutsche from Hungary, though a small number of reliable Moslem officers from the 'Handschar' Division also served. The rank and file were made up of, predominantly Moslem, volunteers. The unit was never actually fully formed and at its peak it reached a maximum strength of just under 9,000 men.

While the division was still working up, it came under threat from the advancing Red Army and the decision was made to allow the rank and file Moslem volunteers to disband and return to their homes. The German cadre personnel were posted to 31.SS-Freiwilligen-Grenadier-Division Böhmen-Mähren and the Moslems who wished to remain in service were transferred to the Handschar Division.

By October 1944 it had been struck from the Order of Battle of the Waffen-SS and its number had been allocated to a Dutch volunteer division which itself never reached greater than regimental strength and was annihilated in the fighting around Berlin in May 1945.

24.Waffen-Gebirgs (Karstjäger) Division der SS

Commanders
SS-Sturmbannführer Berschneider
SS-Sturmbannführer Werner Hahn
SS-Obersturmbannführer Carl Marcks

Main Constituent Units
Waffen-Gebirgsjäger Regiment der SS 59
Waffen-Gebirgsjäger Regiment der SS 60
Gebirgs-Artillerie Regiment 24

This unit originated in the summer of 1942, when Himmler ordered the raising of a mountain troop company to fight in the highest areas of the bare rocky mountainous area on the border between Italy and Yugoslavia. Very soon afterwards the company was expanded to battalion strength. The recruits were mostly local men with extensive knowledge of these mountains.

The Karstjäger (the term 'Karst' refers to the bare, rocky areas in the highest peaks of this mountain region) Battalion was used extensively in anti-partisan operations against the predominantly Communist Italian partisans in the area around Trieste in north-east Italy.

In July 1944 the battalion was ordered to expand to a division. Based in Udine, it was to comprise predominantly Reichsdeutsche from the South Tyrol as well as the original local Italian volunteers. There were problems raising sufficient manpower, and by the end of 1944 it had been decided that a brigade-sized unit might be more feasible; however, even that proved difficult to achieve.

In the closing stages of the war Waffen-Gebirgsjäger-Regiment der SS 59 was heavily engaged in combating elements of the British 8th Army as well as fending off attacks from Italian partisans. It suffered heavily, but fought on determinedly and performed well in difficult circumstances.

The remnants of the unit were combined with

SS-Brigadeführer Otto Kumm, commander of the 7.SS-Gebirgs-Division 'Prinz Eugen' and bearer of the Knights Cross with swords and oakleaves,

THE HIGHER FORMATIONS

In the organisation of German military units in the Second World War, the divisions usually operated as part of a corps, together with at least one other division. The corps usually had its own permanent staff elements, plus support in the form of transport, signals, military police and so on. While the corps structure could be semi-permanent, the divisions controlled by the corps could vary, so

SS-Obergruppenführer Artur Phleps, former general in the Romanian army, was first commander of the 'Prinz Eugen' division, which he led until his death, in 1943.

elements of the 'Prinz Eugen' Division and personnel from the SS-Junkerschule at Klagenfurt in a Kampfgruppe under the command of SS-Brigadeführer Heinz Harmel.

When the bulk of the German forces in Italy surrendered, units in the same area made haste to surrender to the British rather than to the Communist partisans. Harmel and his Kampfgruppe, however, dug in and continued to fight, covering the withdrawal of further German units from Yugoslavia; this certainly saved many German soldiers from falling into the hands of Tito's partisans.

The Karstjäger of the Waffen-SS were among the very last soldiers of the German armed forces to lay down their arms: they finally surrendered to the British on 9 May 1945.

Feldwebel Johann Bauer wears an altered Waffenrock parade dress tunic, together with the marksmanship lanyard. Note the lack of pockets to this tunic. This photograph was taken after the wearing of the Waffenrock had ceased. Bauer appears to have modified his for walking out dress. On the normal Waffenrock the NCO braid to the collar would run along the upper rather than lower edge. (Josef Charita)

On the left is an SS-Obersturmführer from SS-Sturmbrigade 'Wallonie'. Note the army- rather than Waffen-SS-pattern sleeve Edelweiss. (Josef Charita)

that the typical corps headquarters would control two combat divisions, but not always the same two divisions.

The following corps were established to control Gebirgsjäger units of the German armed forces in the Second World War:

V SS-Gebirgskorps Formed in summer 1943 and engaged primarily in anti-partisan operations in the Balkans before being withdrawn into Germany and being destroyed in the battle for Berlin.

IX SS-Gebirgskorps Formed in early 1944 in Croatia; operated in Hungary and was destroyed in the battle for Budapest.

XV Gebirgskorps Formed in summer 1943 and operated in the Balkans; was responsible for the defence of the Dalmatian coast.

XVIII Gebirgskorps Formed in 1938 in Austria and served in the Polish and Western campaigns, the 1941 Balkan campaign and ended the war in the far north of the Eastern Front.

SS-Gebirgsjäger manning a fast assault boat in the waters of an unidentified river in Yugoslavia in 1943/44. Note the shark's-teeth motif painted on the bow of the boat. (Josef Charita)

XIX Gebirgskorps Formed in 1940 and originally entitled Gebirgskorps Norwegen; operated solely on the far northern sector of the Eastern Front; withdrew into Norway at the end of the war.

XXI Gebirgskorps Formed in 1943 in the Balkans; operated in Albania and Yugoslavia and ended the war in the southern sector of the Eastern Front.

XXII Gebirgskorps Formed in 1943 in Greece; operated in the Balkans and in Hungary; ended the war in the southern sector of the Eastern Front.

XXXVI Gebirgskorps Formed in 1939 in Poland; subsequently operated in Norway and the far north of the Eastern Front; withdrew into Norway again at the end of the war.

*An unidentified Waffen-SS Oberscharführer from the anti-tank detachment of an SS Mountain Troop unit. Note the use of the Army pattern metal Edelweiss insignia on the left side of his **Bergmütze** which is fastened with a distinctly non-regulation buckle fitting. (Paul Turner)*

Unteroffizier Georg Audenrieth served in 3 Kompanie, Gebirgsjäger-Regiment 99, part of 1.Gebirgs-Division, and was awarded the Knights Cross of the Iron Cross on 10 February 1945 for gallantry in the face of the enemy. (Audenrieth)

XLIX Gebirgskorps Formed in 1940 in Czechoslovakia; served in the Balkans and the southern sector of the Eastern Front predominantly in the Crimea and the Caucasus, before withdrawing into Czechoslovakia, where it surrendered to the Russians at the end of the war.

LI Gebirgskorps Originally formed as an infantry corps in 1940, it was changed to a Gerbirgskorps and operated on the Eastern Front; lost at Stalingrad.

A number of corps commands were usually controlled by a higher authority at army level.

There was in fact only one mountain army, the 20.Gebirgsarmee, which was formed over the winter of 1941/42 to control the Gebirgskorps, which were operating on the far north of the Eastern Front. In late 1944 it withdrew into Norway, where it absorbed 21.Armee and controlled all German forces based in Norway, before surrendering to the British in 1945.

THE MAJOR CAMPAIGNS

Poland

The 1., 2. and 3.Gebirgs divisions were committed to the campaign against Poland. Their primary objective was the capture of Lemberg in Galicia, the provincial capital and a vital communications link for both rail and road traffic: 1.Gebirgs-Division would strike north from Czechoslovakia; 2.Gebirgs-Division would move eastwards through

Although strictly against regulations, some Luftwaffe personnel based in mountain regions, such as this 88mm anti-aircraft gun crew, also wore the Edelweiss insignia on their caps. (Josef Charita)

Czechoslovakia until it reached the Dukla Pass and then punch north through the pass into Poland; and the elements of 3.Gebirgs-Division that were committed to battle would cover the gap between the other two divisions.

The Gebirgsjäger would be obliged to cross some 200 miles of terrain in order to reach their objectives, and would do so by forced march, since no road or rail transport was available to them. In any case, a good deal of the route crossed mountains and hilly terrain, where travel by foot was the only option.

The Gebirgsjäger made rapid progress, and divisions 1. and 2. swiftly linked up after their pincer movement and rapid punch through Poland. Shortly afterwards 3.Division was removed from the front and despatched westwards.

By 11 September the combined force of divisions 1. and 2. had covered well over 150 miles;

The Narvik Shield. This is an example of the silvered version on field grey backing cloth, as awarded to army personnel. Note the inclusion of an Edelweiss motif in the design, symbolising the participation of the mountain troops in this battle.

Norway

By the early part of 1940, 2. and 3.Gebirgs-Divisions were on the Western Front, poised to strike against France. Then, in March, 3.Gebirgs-Division was withdrawn to Germany to prepare for participation in Hitler's next gambit, a lightning strike against Denmark and Norway. The Gebirgsjäger objective was the port of Narvik in the north of Norway. The mountain soldiers of Gebirgsjäger-Regiment 139 were transported to Narvik by sea, carried by destroyers of the Kriegsmarine. The landing was unopposed and the town was taken without a shot being fired. The divisional commander, Generalleutnant Dietl, accepted the surrender of the local garrison the same day. The success was to be short-lived, however: British warships arrived the following day and the first of a series of naval engagements ensued. The outcome was the sinking of the German destroyer flotilla, with heavy losses, and the British navy laying a blockade around the port. The Germans were now totally cut off from the nearest friendly forces, some 700 miles away.

three days later the Gebirgsjäger were in the hills around Lemberg. A Kampfgruppe from 1.Gebirgs-Division launched an attack on the city while the remaining Gebirgsjäger formed a defensive ring around it to prevent Polish reinforcements, now beginning to arrive in considerable numbers, from relieving Lemberg.

After a battle lasting six days, the Poles surrendered. The Gebirgsjäger were somewhat galled, however, to discover they would have to hand the city over to the Russians, who by then had invaded Poland from the east.

It had been the Gebirgsjäger's first campaign of the war, and they had performed exceptionally well, covering considerable distances in a short time before successfully capturing their objective; they had endured fierce fighting against powerful enemy forces, and had gained the respect of the Polish garrison at Lemberg in the process.

The Lapland Shield. Note the crudity of the cast aluminium construction. It is sewn rather than pinned to its backing cloth.

*The regulation Waffen-SS versions of the Edelweiss insignia for the sleeve (left) and the **Bergmütze**/M43 cap (right). Both are machine-embroidered on a black badge-cloth backing, in silver-grey thread with yellow thread stamens.*

The sunk and beached destroyers were quickly cannibalised for armaments, food and equipment, and the now-redundant survivors among the crews were turned temporarily into soldiers. Now, almost 2,000 sailors would be suddenly available to Dietl.

The Luftwaffe managed to land some transport planes on a nearby frozen lake, and was able to supply Dietl with a small number of 75mm artillery pieces. A defensive ring around most of the port was soon set up, and the men were positioned in small groups, in foxholes blasted out of the bare rock. There were barely enough to cover the perimeter of the port, and Dietl took a calculated risk in not defending the south-eastern

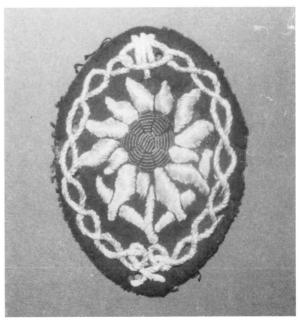

A fine quality hand-embroidered bullion wire version of the army-pattern Edelweiss sleeve patch.

27

A 'flatwire' version of the 'Prinz Eugen' cuff title, woven in aluminium thread on a black rayon base.

The 'Kreta' cuff title, awarded to all who took part in the battle for Crete, in which the Gebirgsjäger, commanded by Julius Ringel, played a decisive part.

The Odal Rune collar patch (here an officers' hand-embroidered aluminium wire version) for the 'Prinz Eugen' division, shown here alongside the standard SS Runes collar patch.

approach to the town, correctly assuming that the terrain there was so difficult as to preclude a British attack from that direction. The British did not attack from the south-east, but a Norwegian force did, and they caused Dietl some considerable worry: they tried to blow the rail and the road links to cut the Germans off, but this attempt was quickly defeated by the Gebirgsjäger.

On 14 April the Norwegian regular army units and elements of the British Expeditionary Force attacked from the north. The weak German force came under considerable pressure, compounded by the Royal Navy sending its destroyers into Narvik Fjord to shell the German positions. Hitler went so far as to give Dietl authority to withdraw his troops into neutral Sweden rather than face defeat, but Dietl refused to give up.

The battle continued, with the Allied side now reinforced by Polish and French troops. The Gebirgsjäger were able to fend off each assault (the Allied attacks were rarely well co-ordinated), but the attrition rate was constantly weakening the German force.

On 27 May, under cover of a naval bombardment, French troops were landed and after bitter, often hand-to-hand, fighting, the town fell to soldiers of the French foreign legion.

A small number of reinforcements, in the form of a few companies of Fallschirmjäger and Jäger troops, were dropped by parachute; welcome though these reinforcements were, it looked certain that the Germans must eventually be defeated, and they awaited the inevitable final assault by the Allies with trepidation.

At the beginning of May the remainder of the division was ordered to proceed to the Narvik area as soon as possible. They were moved from Denmark to Trondheim in Norway, by air, thence to Narvik by a small flotilla of merchant ships with a light naval escort. Unfortunately the flotilla came under attack from British submarines, which

The 'BeVo' version of the cuff title for SS-Gebirgsjäger-Regiment 11 'Reinhard Heydrich', woven in pale grey artificial silk thread on black.

torpedoed two of the transport ships. The remainder of 3.Gebirgs-Division then had to set out on foot, racing against time to cover the 700 miles from Trondheim to Narvik and battling against the rearguard units of retreating Allied formations moving in the general direction of Narvik and against attacks from Norwegian ski-troops.

Despite all the difficulties facing them, leading elements covered almost half the distance to their objectives in just seven days. Time was running out for Dietl's beleaguered force in Narvik, however, and it was decided to make one last all out effort to reach the port by sending one company from each battalion, carrying only light fighting order and leaving all other non-essential kit behind, over the last 130 miles or so, at full speed. The terrain to be covered was a barren wilderness with no roads whatsoever, and the journey was across rivers and glaciers in dreadful weather conditions. When the relief force was but a few days march from Narvik, on 9 June, an order arrived cancelling the operation.

On 8 June Dietl had sent patrols towards the town of Narvik. They had returned to report that the Allies had evacuated their troops. Now, on 9 June, Norway had formally surrendered.

A small group continued its trek and on 13 June made contact with Dietl's force. Dietl and his elite Gebirgsjäger were feted as heroes, and Dietl himself became widely known in Germany as the 'Hero of Narvik'. He was decorated with the Knights Cross of the Iron Cross in recognition of his men's achievements.

France 1940

Only two of the German army's mountain units, 1.Gebirgs-Division and 6.Gebirgs-Division, took part in the French campaign.

1.Gebirgs-Division saw action in the opening phases, and the drive to and over the River Maas. They met no opposition; the division's only casualties were men accidentally drowned in a night crossing of the river. Not until a full week after the invasion did the division finally run into some French opposition, at Rocroi, but this was swiftly overcome.

On reaching the Oisne-Aisne canal, however, the Gebirgsjäger ran into stiffer resistance and came under heavy artillery bombardment. It was forced onto the defensive for about a week. On 5 June, after a massive German artillery barrage on

As light infantry, the Gebirgsjäger usually qualified for the Infanterie Sturmabzeichen after completing three individual combat actions against the enemy. The badge is in white metal or zinc with a vertical pin-back fitting.

Also frequently won by Gebirgsjäger was the Close Combat clasp, shown here in its bronze (bottom), silver (centre) and gold (top) grades for 15, 30 and 50 days close-quarter battle-action respectively.

the French positions, 1.Gebirgs-Division crossed the canal and attacked the French. The resistance was determined, and the French launched immediate counter-attacks. However, the disciplined and determined Gebirgsjäger were able to throw back every attack by their opponents, French colonial troops from Morocco, and eventually the French were forced to retreat; the Gebirgsjäger set off in pursuit. By 7 June the division was crossing the Aisne, and enemy resistance was rapidly crumbling.

It was decided to withdraw the division and send it south to Lyons to hit the rear of the French forces battling the Italians, but the French agreed armistice terms before the division reached its objectives; instead of seeing further action, it went into a period of occupation duties on the border with Switzerland.

It is interesting to note that 1.Gebirgs-Division was selected to become part of the German force which was to have invaded Great Britain in Operation Sealion. After this plan was abandoned, it was to have supplied troops for the intended operation to capture Gibraltar.

The 6.Gebirgs-Division, newly formed, was only able to take part in the very last stages of the battle for France; its duties in this area consisted mainly of occupation service after the armistice.

The Balkans 1941

Following Mussolini's rash decision to invade Greece, in 1940, and the subsequent setbacks his army suffered, especially once British reinforcements had arrived to assist the Greeks, Hitler was unwillingly drawn into the Balkan conflict. Among the divisions committed to the attack in the Balkans in April 1941 were four mountain units: 1.Gebirgs-Division took part in the attack on Yugoslavia, launching its strike from its base area in the Austrian province of Carinthia, 4.Gebirgs-

Division also attacked Yugoslavia from a launch point in Bulgaria; and 5. and 6.Gebirgs-Divisions took part in the invasion of Greece as part of XVIII Gebirgskorps, their task being to smash the Greek defensive system, the Metaxas Line.

The Greek defences posed considerable problems for the Gebirgsjäger. They were well built, well armed and manned by fanatically determined Greek troops. The Gebirgsjäger launched their attack on 6 April. Despite a furious artillery bombardment supplemented by dive bombing attacks from Stukas, by no means all of the Greek strongpoints had been neutralised, and the Germans were forced to take out each pillbox individually. This proved a long and costly process for the lightly armed Gebirgsjäger. Even when positions were finally captured, the Greeks would often put in determined counter-attacks, and it took 5.Gebirgs-Division four days of bitter fighting before they overran the Greek defences.

The 6.Gebirgs-Division was more fortunate, and punched its way through the Greek defences within a single day. The divisions then linked up and fought their way south towards Corinth, against units of the British expeditionary force. By 26 April Athens had fallen; the last of the British forces were withdrawn towards the sea ports of the Peloponnese and evacuated.

In Yugoslavia 1. and 4.Gebirgs divisions fought against a determined Yugoslavian defence in dreadful weather conditions, but the overwhelming strength of the German forces soon saw the Yugoslavs crushed. The total subjugation of Yugoslavia took just 12 days, and both 1. and 4.Gebirgs divisions played a major part in that success, and were congratulated by Hitler himself for their achievements.

The last major engagement in the Balkans in 1941 to involve Gebirgsjäger was the invasion of Crete. General Ringel's 5.Gebirgs-Division was to be transported to Crete (once the Luftwaffe's Fallschirmjäger had been dropped) in a motley flotilla of Greek fishing boats. Unfortunately they were intercepted by British warships, which wreaked havoc on the convoys of small wooden-hulled vessels; losses were considerable.

A second attempt to land Gebirgsjäger on the island was made, this time by air. The mountain

In the group photograph taken on the Eastern Front, the Oberfeldwebel in the centre appears to be wearing the anti-partisan badge in silver on his left breast pocket. Gebirgsjäger often found themselves in action against partisan units, especially in the Balkan theatre. (Ian Jewison)

troopers were landed at Maleme on 22 May by JU 52 transport aircraft. (The transports were forced to land, under fire, on an airstrip littered with the remains of wrecked aircraft.) Once the area around Maleme had been secured by joint Fallschirmjäger/Gebirgsjäger forces, a Gebirgsjäger Kampfgruppe was despatched to drive the New Zealand defenders from the mountains around the airport. After much bitter fighting, which often involved hand-to-hand combat, the Gebirgsjäger began to gain the upper hand, and by 23 May the heights were in German control. With the airport no longer under enemy fire, the Germans could bring in reinforcements, including artillery and heavy equipment. The following week was spent in pursuit of the retreating British and Commonwealth troops who, it seemed to the Gebirgsjäger, were prepared to contest every metre of ground. The New Zealanders, in particular, were to prove determined enemies, and their pugnacious defence cost the Germans dear in casualties. The outcome of the battle was no longer in any doubt, however, and by 31 May

The anti-partisan badge, bronze grade, awarded for 20 individual days combat against partisans.

those British and Commonwealth troops who had not been evacuated by sea surrendered to the Germans.

The Eastern Front

When Operation Barbarossa was launched, in June 1941, the Gebirgsjäger were to play a major part in operations both in the southern and the far northern fronts; in the north, in particular, Gebirgsjäger were prominent among the troops.

Hitler allocated Gebirgskorps Norwegen and XXXVI Korps, together with three corps of the Finnish army, to launch a drive towards the vital port of Murmansk. Gebirgskorps Norwegen was to attack towards the port itself, while the other two corps were to cut the rail link from Murmansk into the Russian heartland.

The terrain in this sector was appalling, comprising a mixture of barren rock and swampland in the north and dank, dark forests to the south, both heavily infested with mosquitoes. The Finns could scarcely believe that the Germans would wish to conduct a campaign in such an area, but Hitler insisted.

Gebirgskorps Norwegen, comprising 2. and 3.Gebirgs-Divisions, made rapid progress at first, despite the atrocious conditions, and smashed through the Russian defences, reaching the River Liza at the beginning of July. By this time, however, the Russians were receiving considerable reinforcements, and the Germans began to meet stiff opposition. The momentum of the advance was slowed drastically and the whole offensive in the north began to falter.

The Russians quickly put in a powerful counter-attack and while this was rebuffed by the Gebirgsjäger, the German advance ran out of steam. With winter approaching, 3.Gebirgs-Division was withdrawn and replaced by 6.Gebirgs-Division.

Further to the south, SS-Kampfgruppe 'Nord', fighting as part of XXXVI Korps, was about to take part in its first major battle. The SS troops had insufficient training and the division was sorely lacking in experienced NCOs. When the SS troops ran into the strongly defended Russian positions, losses were heavy. Where elements were led by experienced officers, progress was initially good, but as soon as these officers became casualties, the advance lost all momentum and the Russians, sensing the German uncertainty, immediately counter-attacked and drove them back. In some cases the badly demoralised SS troops broke and ran. The objectives were eventually taken, but the success was largely due to the German and Finnish army troops on the flanks of the SS-Kampfgruppe.

With the coming of winter, the Soviets launched a major offensive. Although the Germans were severely battered and suffered heavy losses, the line held and over the winter months of 1941-42 a stalemate developed. Only minor skirmishing actions continued as both sides rebuilt their strength for the inevitable battles in the spring.

In early spring 1942, 7.Gebirgs-Division arrived in the far north sector as the Soviets launched their offensive – a combination of massive land forces and a seaborne assault behind the German lines, intended to cut them off. Only after bitter fighting were the Russians held. A second assault wave very nearly succeeded, but then the weather

Service Dress
1: Gebirgsjäger private
2: Gebirgsjäger Hauptmann
3: General der Gebirgstruppe
4: Edelweiss cap badge
5: Gebirgsjäger sleeve patch

A

Parade Dress
1: Jäger private
2: Feldwebel
3: Adjutant

B

Early War, 1940-42
1: Unteroffizier, Gebirgstruppe
2: General der Gebirgstruppe
3: Oberfeldwebel, Crete, 1942

C

Norway/Narvik, 1940
1: Mountain trooper
2: Mountain troop Feldwebel
3: Unteroffizier, Gebirgsjäger

D

Mediterranean Theatre, 1942-44
1: Machine gunner, mountain troop
   regiment
2: Mountain trooper
3: Oberfeldwebel, Italy, 1944
4: Edelweiss *Bergmütze* badge

E

Eastern front, 1942-43
1: Oberfeldwebel
2: Mountain trooper
3: Oberfeldwebel

F

North Russian Front, 1942-44
1: Ski-Jäger Leutnant
2: SS-Schütze, 'Nord' Division
3: Ski-trooper sniper
4: Ski-jäger sleeve patch
5: Ski-jäger cap badge

G

Anti-partisan operations, Balkans, 1943-44
1: Mountain troop machine gunner
2: Waffen-SS unteroffizier
3: SS-Rottenführer, 'Prinz Eugen' Div.
4: Anti-partisan badge

1

2

3

H

Waffen-SS, 'Prinz Eugen' Div.
1: Rottenführer, SS-Gebirgsjäger
2: Hauptsturmführer
3: Untersturmführer
4: SS-pattern sleeve patch

I

Ethnic Waffen SS
1: SS-Sturmbannführer,
   'Handschar' Div.
2: SS-Scharführer, 'Handschar' Div.
3: SS-Hauptsturmführer,
   'Skanderbeg' Div.
4: SS-cap insignia

J

Late War, 1944-45
1: Unteroffizier, Gebirgjäger
2: Kanonier
3: Hauptwachtmeister,
   mountain police
4: Edelweiss arm patch

K

Germany, 1944-45
1: SS-Untersturmführer, 'Nord' Div.
2: SS-Unterscharführer, 'Nord' Div.
3: SS-Rottenführer, 'Kama' Div.
4: SS-pattern cap badge

L

*Page from Paybook (*Soldbuch*) of a Gebirgsjäger NCO, showing his unit attachments. This individual served with Gebirgsjäger Regiment 13, part of 4.Gebirgs-Division.*

closed in with such ferocity that no further military action was possible. By the time weather conditions had improved, the Germans had had time to regroup and better organise their defences, and the Russian offensive failed. Most of 1943 in this sector of the front was spent in minor patrolling activities, both sides having turned their main attention to other sectors of the front.

The summer of 1944 saw fresh Russian offensives against the southern and central sections of the far north sector, but the final collapse was brought about by political rather than military means. In September 1944, the Finns concluded a separate peace with the Russians. The Germans now faced the possibility of attacks from the rear by their own erstwhile allies, and it was decided to pull all German troops in this sector back through Lapland and into Norway.

The Finns carried out several attacks on the retreating Germans, harrying them as they pulled back towards the Norwegian border, but had not the strength to cause the Germans any real prob-

lems. German activity on the far north of the Eastern Front had all but ceased.

On the southern sector of the front, in June 1941, 1. and 4.Gebirgs divisions had taken part in the rapid advances which followed the invasion, driving eastward towards the 'Stalin Line' defences. The attack on these Soviet defence lines by the Gebirgsjäger began on 15 July. After a massive artillery bombardment, the Gebirgsjäger stormed the enemy bunkers. The first line of defences were swiftly overrun, but the speed of the German advance, as on so many occasions, had left gaps in their line, and these were exploited by the Russians, who quickly mounted counter-attacks; bitter hand-to-hand fighting ensued in many places. By 16 July the Germans had penetrated the Stalin Line on a front approximately 15 miles wide. The Russians threw in

Group of officers and senior NCOs, from the 'Prinz Eugen' division. Note cuff titles and the Odal Rune collar patch on the officer on the extreme left.

numerous suicidal attacks, losing huge numbers of men in a desperate attempt to hold back the advancing Germans, while the bulk of the Red Army units withdrew to what they thought was the comparative safety to the east of the River Bug. Indeed, large numbers of Red Army troops made it over the Bug.

By mid-July, however, XLIX Gebirgskorps had crossed the Bug in pursuit of the retreating Russians, before beginning the drive towards Uman. To the north of the Gebirgsjäger, 1.Armee smashed its way forward to Kiev before turning south towards Uman, and in the south 17.Armee, with 1.Armee, formed a gigantic pincer movement that was intended to close behind Uman and encircle the Russians who were retreating before the advance of XLIX Gebirgskorps. This was no simple 'round-up' of a fleeing enemy: the Soviet forces in the Uman pocket were enormous and made concerted efforts to break out but the German lines held and only a small number of

Red Army troops escaped. This was one of the great encirclements of the war in the east, with around 100,000 Red Army prisoners taken, over 20,000 of them by the mountain troops of XLIX Gebirgskorps.

The latter then pushed on towards Stalino, which was captured in the November, before advancing to positions by the River Mius, where they dug in as winter approached.

In July 1942 the Gebirgsjäger took part in a drive south into the Caucasus mountains. German troops in this sector were too few and too widely spread, however, and although Gebirgsjäger succeeded in scaling the highest peak in the Caucasus range, Mount Elbrus, and planted the German flag, powerful Soviet defences prevented much further progress and the massive Soviet counter-attacks which ensued forced the Germans to withdraw. By the end of the year 1. and 4.Gebirgs-Divisions had pulled back into the marshy lands of the Kuban region, a virtual cul-de-sac from which they barely escaped when the Russian offensive in the south was launched following the debacle at Stalingrad.

Meanwhile, on the Leningrad front, 5.Gebirgs-

Division had arrived fresh from its victory in Crete and was put into the line in April 1942, occupying that gloomy, heavily wooded swampland around the River Volkhov. Its prime task was to prevent the escape of Red Army units from the Volkhov pocket.

Fragmented remnants of a number of Red Army units did manage to escape into these great forests, and the Gebirgsjäger had the task of hunting them down through the summer of 1942. As winter approached, the fighting decreased somewhat in intensity, but in the late spring of the following year a massive new Soviet offensive saw the division fragmented as it was battered by hugely superior enemy forces. At the end of the year, 5.Gebirgs-Division was withdrawn and transferred to the southern sector of the front.

As the greatest tank battle of all time unfolded at Kursk in the central sector of the eastern front in the summer of 1943, the Soviets prepared to launch a massive offensive along a 400-mile front in the south. Over 2,500,000 Soviet troops were thrown at a German force only half as strong. On the southern edge of the front the Soviets advanced from the Gulf of Taganrog in mid-

A fascinating and unique presentation casket for the Knights Cross of the Iron Cross in the shape of a mountain-boot, presented to General der Gebirgstruppe Bohme by 7.Gebirgs-Division. The casket has a bronze finish. (P. Pleetinik via F.J. Stephens)

A further view of the presentation casket awarded to General Böhme, with the lid removed to show the Knights Cross. (P. Pleetinik via F.J. Stephens)

August, and by the end of September they were near Melitopol and approaching the Crimea. By the year's end German troops in the Crimea were cut off, and Kiev had been recaptured.

A fresh offensive started in September, continuing the German advance, with over four million troops now being thrown at the Germans, pushing them ever further to the west. By mid-May 1944 the Crimea had been cleared of German troops and the Red Army was approaching the Carpathian mountains. Romania was swiftly overrun, and the Gebirgsjäger were driven back to end the year in Hungary.

Hitler was now desperate to avoid the Soviets overrunning the Hungarian oilfields at Nagykanitzsa, and a German counter-attack was planned. By this point, 1.Gebirgs-Division was part of 2.Panzerarmee, which was to form the southern prong of a two-pronged attack. The offensive, around the area of the Platensee, started on 5 March, but the spring thaw had turned the terrain into a veritable sea of mud, and the heavier vehicles became bogged down almost immediately. Light infantry such as the Gebirgsjäger could still move, however, and for

the first ten days or so of the offensive, the mountain troops made good progress. Soon even they began to falter, and the advance petered out. On 21 March a massive new Russian counter-attack began and the German line began to crumble immediately. Over 40 Red Army divisions faced a mere handful of German units, including 1.Gebirgs-Division and 13.Waffen-Gebirgs-Division der SS 'Handschar'.

Both 2.Panzerarmee and 6.SS Panzerarmee to the north were forced to retreat. Such was the reputation of 1.Gebirgs-Division for reliability and steadfastness that it was ordered to provide the rearguard, holding back the Soviet horde while the bulk of the German forces withdrew westwards.

In the last few weeks of the war, 1. and 9.Gebirgs-Divisions were fighting in the Steiermark area of Austria, fragmented into small battle groups which fought numerous last-ditch actions against the Red Army before being forced to surrender in May 1945.

Further north, 4.Gebirgs-Division had been driven back into Slovakia, where it became part of another notional 'armoured' force, 1.Panzerarmee. These so-called 'tank armies' had, by then, precious few armoured vehicles remaining. (1.Panzerarmee also went into Soviet captivity when the war ended.)

The base of General Bohme's casket has an engraved dedication plate and the interior of the lid bears a numeral 7 for 7 Gebirgs-Division. (P. Pleetinik via F.J. Stephens)

Further to the north, 3.Gebirgs-Division had also been forced back and was fighting in Upper Silesia when it was finally forced to surrender.

Somewhat more fortunate in their fates were Gebirgs-Divisions 5 and 8, which were operating in Italy. 5.Gebirgs-Division had been put into the line south of Rome in 1943 and took part in the fighting retreat up through Italy as part of LI Gebirgskorps. In the final stages of the war, it fought in the defence of the Gothic Line, before surrendering to British forces in the north-west of Italy in late 1944. 8.Gebirgs-Division saw action in Italy in the area around Bologna, as part of XIV Korps. It was driven back as far as the Po Valley, eventually surrendering to the Americans in the north-west of Italy in late 1944.

Divisions, 2, 6 and 7, which had withdrawn into Norway, were still there when the war ended and they surrendered to the British.

The Western Front

The only major involvement of mountain troop units on the Western Front in the second half of the war was during Operation Northwind. This was launched after the failure of the Ardennes offensive, as the Germans tried to relieve Allied pressure in the Ardennes by launching an attempt to drive through the American lines in the south and recapture Strasbourg. Elements of 6.SS-Gebirgs-Division 'Nord' were involved in the attempt to cross the River Moder and drive through into the Vosges region, Although the SS troops fared well, much better in fact than they had done on the Eastern Front, being by now seasoned veterans, the offensive was doomed. Launched at the beginning of January, it began to run out of steam within a few days, though the mountain troops of the 'Nord' Division did succeed in decimating the US 45th Division with relatively few losses to themselves. It then had the task of crossing the River Ruwer, supported by 2.Gebirgs-Division, and retaking Trier. In the bloody battle which ensued, the mountain troops were forced back, but not without inflicting extremely heavy losses on the Americans.

Ironically, 'Nord', after such an unimpressive start in combat on the far north of the Eastern Front, was by now the best unit available to the

Major Friedrich Bader, showing a fine range of combat decorations. Note the Heeresbergführer badge, below the German Cross on the right breast pocket, and the Croat Order of King Zvonimir, below the Iron Cross on the left breast pocket. The Honour Roll clasp on the ribbon of the Iron Cross Second Class in the tunic buttonhole has been mounted upside-down, with the ribbon bow to the oakleaf wreath at the top rather than the bottom. For some unknown reason the Close Combat clasp above his left breast pocket has also been mounted upside-down. Note the use of metal rather than cloth cap insignia. (Josef Charita)

Guerrilla War in the Balkans

In virtually every country occupied by the Germans during the Second World War, guerrilla movements of some kind sprang up. In occupied Yugoslavia, the Germans faced two distinct resistance groups: the Royalist Chetniks and Tito's Communist partisans. (The two groups hated each other almost as much as they hated the Germans.) Initially, partisan activity was not too serious a problem, but Tito soon organised his partisans along formal military lines. Disciplined and well trained, they grew steadily, soon numbering over 150,000.

When Italy capitulated in 1943, the Italian troops in Yugoslavia were withdrawn and many simply abandoned their weapons and heavy equipment. These were quickly snatched by Tito's partisans. Allied air-drops of supplies and equipment gave the partisans an even greater offensive capability.

The 7.SS-Freiwilligen-Gebirgs-Division 'Prinz Eugen' was raised specifically to combat the partisan menace in Yugoslavia. It first saw action in January 1943 in a major anti-partisan drive lasting until March, and shortly thereafter helped round up the remaining Italian troops still on Yugoslavian soil. 'Prinz Eugen' also assisted with the raising and training of the 13.Waffen-Gebirgs-Division der SS 'Handschar'.

In May 1944 the division took part in a major offensive aimed at capturing Tito and smashing the partisans, now known as the Yugoslav National Army of Liberation. Although Tito's headquarters at Drvar was captured, Tito himself escaped by the skin of his teeth. Several partisan divisions were decimated in the fighting, though losses were heavy on both sides and the partisans proved themselves brave and skilful opponents.

In the spring of 1944 the entire military balance in the area was changed when both Bulgaria and Romania changed sides and, together with massive Red Army forces, began a drive towards Belgrade. Soon the 'Prinz Eugen' Division found itself fighting not just partisans but front line enemy combat divisions.

'Prinz Eugen' was active in the area around Nish, covering the withdrawal of Heeresgruppe E, before it began its own retreat westwards.

Germans on the southern part of the Western Front, and it gave good service, covering the retreat of most of the remaining German forces over the Rhine before attempting to escape itself. It was too late for most of the SS troops, however. Only a few managed to escape into German-held territory; the remainder became American captives.

During the last few months of the war, the division was used as a 'fire brigade', being rushed from one crisis spot to another as one of the few divisions still available which could be depended upon to continue to fight with absolute determination no matter what the odds. It formed the rearguard of the German retreat from the Balkans into Austria, and fought to the last, before being forced to surrender to the partisans on 16 May 1945. Many of the division's personnel were killed by the partisans.

UNIFORMS AND INSIGNIA

Headgear

The headgear worn by the Gebirgsjäger of the German army was, almost without exception, the standard headgear issued to all other branches of the service.

Features which distinguished headgear as Gebirgsjäger issue included the use of light green coloured piping to the crown and band of the peaked cap or *Schirmmütze*, and on the tropical peaked field cap an inverted chevron of light green coloured 'Russia braid' which enclosed the national colours cockade insignia. In addition, between the eagle and swastika national emblem to the front of the peaked cap, and the wreathed national colours cockade on the cap band, was pinned a small white metal stemless Edelweiss insignia. On the left hand side of the field cap was pinned, or sewn, a white metal or zinc Edelweiss, with stem. The one piece of headgear specific to Gebirgsjäger was the *Bergmütze* or mountain cap, closely modelled on the mountain cap as worn by Austrian mountain troops in the First World War. It was cut from field grey wool or tricot and had side flaps which could be folded down to cover the ears and back of the head in bad weather. These flaps buttoned under the wearer's chin and when not in use were fastened at the front of the cap, which also featured a short peak.

Insignia on the front of the *Bergmütze* consisted

Major Ludwig Stautner of Gebirgsjäger Regiment 139. A veteran of the First World War, he wears the 1914 Iron Cross in both grades, to which the 1939 clasp has been added. Note also the Imperial German-pattern wound badge. The Heeresbergführer badge can be seen to good effect in this shot. (Josef Charita)

of an eagle and swastika over a national colours cockade, all woven in pale grey artificial silk on a green T-shaped backing.

The metal-stemmed Edelweiss insignia was worn on the left side flap.

A white cover was also produced for the *Bergmütze* as camouflage when operating in snowy terrain.

So popular was the *Bergmütze* that in 1943 a new general issue field cap for all branches of the armed forces, the *Einheitsfeldmütze Modell 1943*, was introduced. It was an almost exact copy of the

A group of mountain troopers from 7.SS-Freiwilligen-Gebirgs-Division 'Prinz Eugen'. The Odal Rune collar patch, Edelweiss arm patch and divisional cuff band are worn. Unusually, the SS-Sturmmann, on the extreme left, has added rank insignia and a cuff title to his denim fatigue jacket. (Paul Turner)

Bergmütze but with a longer peak, and it replaced the *Bergmütze*.

Waffen-SS mountain troops had, like their army counterparts, specific identifying features for their headgear. Light green piping was occasionally used on the peaked cap (Schirmmütze) but this was by no means common. Confusing and contradictory orders were issued about the use of coloured piping on Waffen-SS peaked caps: coloured piping was only authorised for a very short period before being prohibited again, but those who had already obtained hats with coloured piping seem to have continued wearing them. White piping was the official branch colour for

headgear piping for all Waffen-SS units, but original examples of such headgear with green piping do appear from time to time. The small, metal, stemless Edelweiss worn on army *Schirmmützen* was not, however, authorised for use on Waffen-SS peaked caps.

Waffen-SS mountain troops also used the *Bergmütze* and the M43 field cap. Insignia on these caps initially consisted of a woven artificial silk deaths head in pale grey on black to the front of the cap, with an eagle and swastika in the same colours on the left side flap. With the Edelweiss badge, which in the case of SS caps was embroidered, also added to the left side flap, the side of the cap looked rather cluttered. Caps were often worn with a single rather than the more normal two-button fastening as found on army caps. This exposed a greater area of the front of the cap and allowed both the deaths head and eagle to be worn at the front of the cap and Edelweiss only on the left side flap. Ultimately a new style of insignia was introduced with both the eagle and the deaths head in pale grey thread on a single trap-ezoidal field grey backing.

Mountain troops also wore a peaked field cap, similar to the M43 style but cut from camouflage-pattern cotton duck. Early patterns were non-reversible, but a second model had predominantly green camouflaged patterns on one side, reversible to a predominantly brown pattern on the other. Although appropriately coloured insignia were produced for these caps, it seems, from photographic evidence, to have been only very rarely worn.

Since many of the mountain troop personnel of the Waffen-SS were non-German volunteers of the Moslem religion, Himmler authorised the wearing of the fez by these troops. The Waffen-SS fez was a very simple piece of head-wear, made from pressed felt, without a lining and featuring a leather or artificial leather sweatband and a black cord 'tassel'. It was made in a burgundy colour material for dress wear and field grey for field wear. Insignia consisted of the standard machine-woven eagle and deaths head badges.

The majority of forms of dress worn by the Gebirgsjäger of both the army and Waffen-SS — combat dress, parade dress, walking out dress and so on – were standard-issue garments as worn by all other branches. The following features identified them as Gebirgsjäger.

Army Uniform

Light green underlay to the collar and cuff patches on the Waffenrock parade dress for both officers and other ranks.

Light green underlay to officers' shoulder straps.

Light green piping to NCOs' and other ranks' shoulder straps.

Light green strip of Waffenfarbe colouring to the centre of each bar of the officers' collar patch, and the earlier issues of NCO/other ranks collar patches.

Light green piping to the front, collar, cuffs and rear skirt of the Waffenrock parade dress tunic and to the front and collar of many privately purchased walking out dress tunics. Light green piping to the outer seam on the leg of parade dress and walking out dress trousers.

Light green backing to the flags in the standard bearer's arm patch. The Edelweiss mountain troopers arm patch. This was initially either machine-woven or machine-embroidered, with a green stem, white petals, yellow stamens and a silver-grey twisted rope-effect border, all on a dark green backing. The backing changed to a field grey colour on some wartime patterns, but most Gebirgsjäger seem to have continued to wear the earlier pattern.

Officers occasionally wore hand-embroidered bullion wire versions of the Edelweiss. Examples also exist on a tan coloured backing, but some doubt still exists as to the originality of these. (Ski-Jäger were considered part of the Jäger rather than the Gebirgsjäger branch. They wore the same light green piping where appropriate, but the badge worn on the left flap of the field cap consisted of a spray of three oakleaves – the Jäger badge – with a ski overlaid diagonally on the oakleaves. The arm patch consisted of a spray of three green oakleaves with brown stems, all on a dark green backing with a bright green twisted rope effect border. Laid over this diagonally was a ski in white thread. The entire badge was woven in artificial silk thread.)

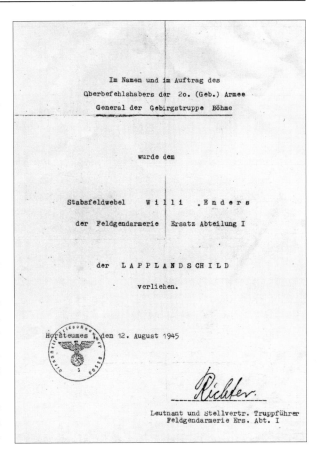

The award document for the Lapland Shield, in this case to a senior NCO in the military police attached to 20.Gebirgsarmee in Norway. Note that the date of the award is after the end of the war. By this time most official documents had been 'de-nazified' by having the swastika on all ink stamps deleted. This document has been authenticated by an unaltered stamp.

Waffen-SS Uniform

Light green piping to NCOs' and other ranks' shoulder straps.

Light green intermediate underlay on officers' shoulder straps.

Mountain troops arm patch consisting of a black oval backing with silver-grey thread border containing a silver-grey thread Edelweiss with yellow thread stamens.

Some of the Waffen-SS Gebirgsjäger units also had collar patches or cuff-titles specific to them. A large number of Waffen-SS collar patches were designed and manufactured but never issued. The following are those which are known, from photographic evidence, to have been widely worn.

6. SS-Gebirgs-Division 'Nord'

As a German division, this unit wore the SS runes on the collar patch.

Cuff-titles were authorised and worn by the regiments 'Reinhard Heydrich' and 'Michael Gaissmair'. The former was manufactured in a number of forms – machine-embroidered silver-grey thread on a black woven band with woven aluminium thread edging (generally known to collectors as the 'RZM' style); machine-woven in aluminium wire thread on a black woven band with woven aluminium thread edging (generally referred to as the 'flat-wire' pattern); and machine-woven in a single operation in grey artificial silk thread on black (universally known as the 'BeVo' pattern). The 'Michael Gaissmair' cuff-title, however, is only known in the 'BeVo' pattern, and this pattern was worn by all ranks.

7. SS-Freiwilligen-Gebirgs-Division 'Prinz Eugen'

As a principally ethnic German unit, this division wore the so-called 'Odal Rune' on its collar patch rather than the normal SS runes. Those members who were German nationals, and thus full members of the SS, could wear a set of bullion thread embroidered SS runes on the left breast pocket.

Only a divisional title is known to have been worn. It has appeared in the 'RZM' and 'Flatwire' types but not in 'BeVo'. A machine-woven version is known, but is woven in fine silver-grey silk thread on black with its own characteristic lettering style. This type is known as the 'BeVo like' pattern.

13. Waffen-Gebirgs-Division der SS 'Handschar'

As a non-German volunteer unit, this division was not permitted the SS runic collar patch. Instead the right hand collar patch displayed a hand grasping a scimitar with a small swastika on the lower left side of the patch, under the Scimitar blade. Once again, German cadre personnel could wear the SS runes on the breast pocket.

The Croat national arm shield – a heraldic shield with a red and white chequered field was worn by many divisional personnel, below the sleeve eagle on the left sleeve.

21. Waffen-Gebirgs-Division der SS 'Skanderbeg'

A special collar patch was designed and manufactured for the members of this predominantly Moslem, Albanian volunteer division but it does not appear to have been issued. German cadre personnel wore the standard SS runes while Albanian volunteers wore a plain blank patch.

A cuff-band in the 'BeVo like' pattern was issued, as was a special arm shield showing a black Albanian double-headed eagle on a red field.

23. Waffen-Gebirgs-Division der SS 'Kama'

A special collar patch was designed and manufactured for this division, showing a simple stylised sunflower motif, but it does not appear to have been issued. SS runes were worn by German cadre personnel and a plain blank patch by the Croat volunteer personnel.

24. Waffen-Gebirgs-Division der SS

A special collar patch bearing a so-called Karst flower motif was designed and probably manufactured, but was never issued to the division's personnel. No cuff-band or other special insignia was produced.

Special Mountain Troops Clothing

In addition to the normal forms of dress worn by all Wehrmacht personnel, mountain troops made wide use of cold-weather clothing, some of which was specific to their branch of the service.

Standard winter clothing included the padded winter suit. This was a heavy padded double-breasted jacket with hood attached. It was reversible, with grey or camouflage pattern on one side and white on the other. It had two large skirt pockets that gave access to the clothing underneath. With this jacket were worn a pair of matching overtrousers.

More specific to the Gebirgsjäger was the wind jacket, a lightweight waterproof cotton jacket intended for wear over the service tunic. It was double-breasted and olive green in colour (non-reversible). It had two skirt pockets, a half-belt at the rear and two slanted 'muff' pockets. The ends of the sleeves had strap adjustments to tighten the fit in cold weather. The Edelweiss arm patch was often worn, and the jacket was fitted with loops at the shoulder seam to take shoulder straps.

In 1942 an anorak with matching trousers was also introduced for Gebirgsjäger. It was in typical pullover style, with attached hood and a large, button-down flap covering to the neck opening. It had a large three-section pocket across the chest and a 'tail' strap attached to the rear of the skirt which could be passed through the wearer's legs and fastened to a button on the skirt front. There were also two rear pockets on the lower skirt. The anorak had a drawstring waist and adjustable tapes on the cuffs. Overtrousers were supplied with the anorak and had a drawstring waist fitting. The anorak and trousers were reversible from grey to white.

Although the standard jackboot and ankle-boot did see service with mountain troop personnel, when operating in mountain terrain the mountain-boot was used. This was an ankle-boot with double thickness sole. As well as the usual hob-nails in the sole and heel of the boot, the edges to the sole and heel were also fitted with studs, in pairs spaced around the sole, and all around the heel. It was lace fastened, through five pairs of eyelets, with four pairs of hooks above the eyelets. The boot was usually used in conjunction with mountain trousers and puttees.

The mountain trouser was similar to standard army trousers, but had a fairly wide leg, tapered at the bottom to allow it to be tucked into the mountain-boot. Each leg had a slash at the bottom for adjustment and was fitted with securing tapes. The seat and inside of the legs were reinforced.

The puttee was made from grey-green woollen cloth some 30 inches long, and was pointed at one end, with a small strap-and-buckle fastening. Once fully wound on, the pointed end was visible on the outside of the ankle, with the point towards the rear.

With the standard ankle-boot, greyish brown canvas gaiters could be worn. These were attached by two leather straps which were worn to the outside of the ankle when the gaiters were fitted.

Awards and Other Special Badges

As light infantry, Gebirgsjäger were eligible for the award of the Infantry Assault Badge in Silver, after taking part in three separate engagements with the enemy. They were also eligible for the Close Combat Clasp in Bronze after 15 days of close quarter battle, in Silver after 30 days and Gold after 50 days.

There were no combat badges produced specifically for Gebirgsjäger, but there were a number of campaign and other decorations which, although not specifically intended for Gebirgsjäger, were awarded to mountain troops in considerable numbers.

The Narvik Shield

Instituted on 19 August 1940 to recognise those personnel who had taken part in the battle for Narvik.

The award took the form of a shield with an eagle and swastika with folded wings at the top, over a panel bearing the title 'Narvik'. Below this, on the main field, was the date 1940 and motifs representing the three branches of the services involved – an Edelweiss for the Gebirgsjäger, a propeller for the Luftwaffe and an anchor for the navy. As worn by Gebirgsjäger it was in a silvered finish and attached to a field grey backing cloth to allow it to be stitched to the upper left sleeve.

Of 8577 awarded, 2755 were to Gebirgsjäger.

The Lapland Shield

Authorised by the commander of 20.Gebirgsarmee, General der Gebirgstruppe Bohme, the Lapland Shield was the last German decoration of the Second World War; in fact its issue did not take place until after the war had ended.

The shield showed a relief map of the Lapland region, with the title 'Lappland' above, and at the top of the shield an eagle with folded wings and no swastika. As the shield did not feature this (by then) prohibited emblem, the British forces in Norway, to whom the Germans had surrendered at the end of the war, allowed the manufacture of this shield and its distribution to the troops. (It is unlikely, however, that any would actually have been worn, and that they were simply preserved by their recipients as commemorative pieces.) They were extremely crudely manufactured, usually cast in aluminium, though some were simply etched onto a piece of flat aluminium sheet.

The Kreta Cuff-band

Instituted on 16 October 1942 to reward those who had taken part in the battle for Crete, in which of course the Gebirgsjäger played a significant role, this award consisted of a white cloth band with golden yellow Russia Braid edging. In the centre was the legend 'Kreta', flanked on either side by a spray of acanthus leaves. It was worn on the lower left sleeve.

The Anti-Partisan Badge

Not strictly a Gebirgsjäger award, but in view of the role played by mountain divisions, especially those of the Waffen-SS, in the anti-partisan war in the Balkans, it is one for which many Gebirgsjäger would have qualified.

It was instituted by Himmler in January 1944, and consisted of a vertical wreath of oakleaves with a deaths head device at the base. In the centre was a writhing multi-headed serpent into which a sword was plunged. The sword bears a 'sunwheel' swastika on its hilt. It was awarded in bronze finish for 20 days anti-partisan combat service, silver for 50 days and gold for 150 days.

On the back was a vertical hinged pin fitting. Authenticated examples have been encountered with both needle and wide flat pins, and with the reverse face either solid or semi-hollow struck.

The Heeresbergführer Badge

Instituted in August 1936 to recognise those personnel who were qualified mountain guides, this badge consists of an enamelled metal oval with white outer border and green central field onto which is mounted a silvered Edelweiss with gilt stamens.

At the base is the title 'Heeresbergführer' in gothic characters. It was to have been worn on the left breast pocket, but seems also to have been commonly worn on the right.

Unofficial Awards

In addition to the various national level military awards that were awarded, many individual divisions, regiments and even companies instituted their own, strictly unofficial, commemorative awards. A number are known which relate specifically to mountain units.

Commemorative Medal for the Caucasus

Type 1: The obverse bears a representation of mountain peaks over an Edelweiss flower. Above is the legend 'Kaukasuseinsatz' and below '13/Geb.Jag.Rgt.98'. The reverse bears the names of the battles in which the unit fought – Kluchorpass, Glitschal, Gunailatal and Schemacho, all over the year 1942. The medal is struck in zinc and was produced for 13 Kompanie, Gebirgsjäger-Regiment 98, part of 1.Gebirgs-Division.

Type 2: The obverse of this version bears a representation of mountain peaks over which flies a pennant in the design of the Reichskriegsflagge. At the top is the legend 'Kaukasus 1942'. The reverse bears the tactical symbol of the unit over which is superimposed an Edelweiss. This medal was produced for Gebirgs-Nachrichten Abteilung 54, also a part of 1.Gebirgs-Division.

Medal to Commemorate the Polar Front 1942/43

This medal is in blackened zinc. On the obverse is the Edelweiss and on the reverse at the top, the year '1942' followed by the legend 'Eismeerfront' in pseudo-gothic characters, and at the bottom, the year '1943'. It is not known to which specific unit this medal relates.

THE PLATES

Service Dress
A1: Private, Gebirgsjäger
The Gebirgsjäger private is wearing normal everyday service dress. His steel helmet is the M35 pattern with insignia decals. The tunic worn is the M36 pattern in good quality field grey wool. The insignia is the early pattern in machine-woven artificial silk threads. Both collar patches and shoulder straps bear the light green piping colour of Jäger troops. The trousers are in the so-called 'stone grey' colour, this was later replaced with field grey due to the demand for standardisation in the wartime economy; they are tucked into standard-issue marching boots. He wears the standard black leather waistbelt, with aluminium

finish buckle, to which has been added the triple pocket ammunition pouches for his Mauser 7.92mm Kar 98k carbine. The standard-issue bayonet is worn from a black leather frog.

A2: Hauptmann, Gebirgsjäger

This Hauptmann of Gebirgsjäger wears the officers' tunic with dark green collar, but with the earlier eight-button front fastening and slash, rather than patch, lower pockets – common features of officer tunics in the Reichswehr period. His insignia is in fine quality hand-embroidered aluminium wire. The standard officers' service belt in brown leather and with double claw buckle is worn. His officers' breeches are also in the early, stone grey colour and are worn with highly polished officers' riding boots. Headgear is the peaked cap, or *Schirmmütze*, identified as Gebirgsjäger by the light green piping to the crown and band and the small white metal Edelweiss motif.

A3: General der Gebirgstruppe

The piped service tunic worn by this general of mountain troops shows bright red generals' piping rather than the light green of the Gebirgsjäger. His status as General der Gebirgstruppe is shown by the Edelweiss arm patch and white metal Edelweiss motif on the cap. Underlay to the collar patches and shoulder straps is also in bright red, as are the broad 'lampassen' stripes to the outer seam of his stone grey breeches. His peaked cap bears gilt piping to the crown and band, and gilt aluminium braid cap cords. The insignia, however, are embroidered in silver wire. His brown leather belt bears the same style of buckle as the standard officers' belt, but in matt gilt finish.

A4: Edelweiss cap badge

This small white metal Edelweiss is worn below the eagle and swastika national emblem on the peaked cap (see *A1* and *A2*). It was introduced in May 1939.

A5: Gebirgsjäger sleeve patch

Made to a standard machine woven pattern, the Gebirgsjäger sleeve patch, introduced in 1939, was worn by all ranks.

Parade Dress

B1: Jäger, Gebirgsjäger Regt. 98

The *Waffenrock* or parade dress jacket is being worn by this Jager. Note that the front of the jacket, collar and cuffs are all piped in light green. The collar patches and cuff patches are mounted on light green backing material and on his right upper sleeve is the Edelweiss sleeve patch of the Gebirgsjäger.

All buttons are in bright aluminium finish, and the breast eagle is woven in bright aluminium thread. His regimental number '98' is embroidered into the dark green shoulder straps, in light green thread. His trousers, tucked into his jackboots, are in stone grey wool and have light green piping to the outer seam. His helmet, as was common for parade wear, is in a light grey green smooth paint finish. Combat helmets were usually of a darker shade, with a rough paint finish.

B2: Feldwebel, Gebirgsjäger Regt. 99

This Feldwebel's *Waffenrock* tunic is identified as an NCO pattern by the wide aluminium braid trim to the collar and cuffs, as well as to the shoulder straps, which bear aluminium numerals, '99', and a single rank pip. On the right sleeve, as well as the Gebirgsjäger arm patch, is the standard bearers' insignia. This is worn below the Edelweiss patch. It consists of a machine-woven national emblem in black thread with white highlights, superimposed on two crossed banners featuring the light green field for Jäger troops, all over a sprig of oakleaves. Across the shoulder he wears a leather bandoleer, faced with aluminium braid with a central stripe of light green.

B3: Hauptmann, Gebirgsjäger Regt. 136

This officer's *Waffenrock* dress is basically similar to that worn by lower ranks, but in finer quality materials and with heavy hand-embroidered aluminium wire insignia. His status as adjutant is shown by his aluminium braid aiguillettes. His shoulder strap numerals identify him as belonging to Gebirgsjäger-Regiment 136, part of 2.Gebirgs-Division. The officers' parade belt is in fine aluminium brocade with green stripes, and has an aluminium buckle. The steel helmet was common parade wear for officers as well as lower ranks.

Early War, 1940-42

C1: Unteroffizier, Gebirgsjäger Regt. 98, 1939

This Unteroffizier shows the typical appearance of the Gebirgsjäger in normal service dress around the outbreak of war. The stone grey trousers are still evident, having not yet been replaced by field grey issues.

His belt buckle is now finished in field grey rather than bright aluminium, and his steel helmet has a darker, rougher paint finish. Although not visible, on his waistbelt are the triple pocket ammunition pouches for his Mauser Kar 98k carbine, and he wears black leather 'Y'-strap equipment suspenders. He still wears the regimental number on his shoulder strap, but now on a separate, removable cloth slide.

C2: General der Gebirgstruppe Dietl, 1940

Puttees were favoured by General der Gebirgstruppe Dietl, worn to just below the knee, in conjunction with his general's breeches. This view shows him just after the battle of Narvik. (Note that he wears the Knights Cross and Narvik Shield awarded to him for his part in that battle.) His tunic is the basic M1936 officers' pattern, but with generals' rank insignia, gilt buttons and red generals' piping to the front and to the edges of the turn-back cuffs. His generals' version of the *Bergmütze* had gilt piping to the crown and gilt buttons fastening the side flaps.

C3: Oberfeldwebel, Crete, 1942

This Oberfeldwebel fighting on Crete in 1942 wears the black leather mountain-boots with canvas gaiters into which he has tucked his field grey mountain trousers. His tunic is a simplified version of the M1936 pattern, which though still featuring the dark green collar, has plain unpleated pockets with straight rather than scalloped flaps. The breast eagle is now in grey rather than white thread on dark green backing and his collar patches are general-issue type, lacking the light green Waffenfarbe colour to each bar. As an NCO his collar is trimmed in aluminium braid. The other ranks' version of the *Bergmütze* is worn. The insignia is woven on a T-shaped backing and on the side of the cap is the grey metal Edelweiss insignia.

Narvik, Norway, 1940

D1: Private, Gebirgsjäger Regt. 136

This mountain troop private wears the standard-issue greatcoat for duties in cold climate or in the winter months. Note the puttees worn with the mountain-boot and the boot's heavily studded double-thickness sole. He carries the standard Kar 98k, the most widely used infantry weapon of the German armed forces in the Second World War. Circa 1940, his helmet still bears the national colours decal on the right side, a feature that was soon to be deleted.

D2: Feldwebel, Gebirgsjäger Regt. 137

This mountain troop NCO wears light fighting order with his M1936-pattern tunic and mountain trousers The tunic carries NCO braid to the collar and to the edges of the shoulder straps. The popular *Bergmütze* is worn, with its edelweiss insignia on the left flap, together with snow goggles. Once again the ubiquitous Kar 98k is the weapon carried.

D3: Unteroffizier, Gebirgsjäger Regt. 139

During the battle for Narvik, a number of Gebirgsjäger reinforcements were dropped by parachute to reinforce General Dietl's beleaguered forces. This NCO wears normal M1936 service dress with mountain trousers, but with the standard-issue Luftwaffe paratroopers' smock over his normal clothing, hence the Luftwaffe breast eagle carried on the smock. He also wears the Luftwaffe paratroopers' steel helmet, though the NCO carries his *Bergmütze* tucked into his belt. The weapon here is the MP38 machine-pistol for which two triple pocket, canvas ammunition pouches are worn.

Mediterranean theatre, 1942-44

E1: Gefreiter, Gebirgsjäger Regt. 85, Italy, Spring 1944

This machine-gunner from a mountain troop regiment wears the anorak with its grey side outermost, and with the tail strap between the legs fastened. Field grey mountain trousers are worn along with puttees and mountain-boots. His weapon is an MG34 machine-gun and on his belt he wears the machine-gunners' pouch containing cleaning kit, stripping tools and so on. He also carries a 9mm pistol in a leather holster on his belt. His steel helmet is the M42 pattern without insignia decals.

E2: Jäger, Gebirgsjäger Regt. 100, Italy, Summer 1944

Operating in the Mediterranean theatre, this mountain trooper wears full tropical kit. The usual mountain-boots are worn, with ankle put-tees, in conjunction with tropical trousers of typical baggy cut. He also wears the tropical field blouse similar to that worn by the Afrikakorps but with plain unpleated pockets having a straight rather than scalloped flap. The tunic collar and the shoulder straps have golden brown coloured NCO braid edging.

His belt and Y-straps are made from olive green webbing material but have the standard black leather ammunition pouches for his Mauser Kar 98k carbine. His belt buckle is painted in an olive brown colour. He wears a tropical field cap with the cockade emblem enclosed by a chevron of light green piping. (This was no longer being added to new production caps, but many owners continued to wear the coloured chevron after it had been deleted by regulation.) His mountain troops' sleeve patch is woven on a tan backing. This is still rather contentious: although original examples apparently exist, there is still some debate as to whether or not such insignia was genuinely manufactured and issued during wartime.

E3: Oberfeldwebel, Gebirgjäger Regt. 100, Italy 1944

This feldwebel is from a mountain troop unit operating in Italy in 1944. He wears the standard mountain-boots, but with socks rolled down over the tops of the boots, rather than using gaiters or puttees. He wears shorts cut from a pale olive green denim-type material, and a lightweight reed green denim summer tunic. The braid on his col-lar is woven in mouse-grey silk rather than aluminium braid.

The breast eagle and collar patches are woven in the same mouse-grey shade. Shoulder straps are now cut from a field grey rather than dark green

cloth. The standard black leather waist belt and field grey painted buckle are worn, together with a black leather P38 pistol holster and map case. The *Bergmütze*, by then, had been largely replaced by the M43 field cap shown here, but the metal edel-weiss badge on the side flap remained.

E4: Edelweiss **Bergmütze** badge

This is an example of the metal edelweiss badges worn on the side of the cap.

Eastern Front, 1942-43
F1: Oberfeldwebel, Gebirgsjäger Regt. 138, south Russian Front, Autumn 1942

The standard-issue mountain troop windjacket is being worn by this Oberfeldwebel. It was designed to be worn over the normal field blouse and is fit-ted with shoulder straps. The usual black leather belt and Y-straps are being worn, together with the large, well packed mountain troops' rucksack. The NCO carries the MP38 machine pistol with its attendant ammunition pouches on his belt. As its name suggests, the windjacket was to help alle-viate the wind-chill factor at high altitudes, but was a lightweight garment which in itself did not give any great protection from the cold. The stan-dard *Bergmütze* is being worn.

F2: Jäger, Gebirgsjäger Regt. 91, Caucasus Mountains, Winter 1942

In the terrible sub-zero temperatures of the Eastern Front, this mountain trooper wears the heavy padded reversible clothing, which has no visible rank insignia, with its white side outer-most. The jacket has an integral hood, and access to the uniform underneath via the pockets. His steel helmet has been whitewashed to give added camouflage in snowy terrain. Although heavy padded mittens were also produced, this particular soldier has retained the normal field green knitted wool gloves.

F3: Oberfeldwebel, 1. Ski-Jäger Brigade, January 1943

This ski-trooper wears the standard reversible grey-to-white anorak, with the white side outer-most, together with white overtrousers and mountain-boots which were purpose-designed to be suitable for use with skis. White padded mittens are worn. These were designed with a 'finger' for the trigger finger to allow him to fire his weapon without removing the mittens. The normal black leather belt is worn, with canvas pouches for his machine pistol. These pouches have been smeared with whitewash to aid concealment. Even his *Bergmütze* has a removable white camouflaged cover.

North Russian Front, 1942-44
G1: Leutnant, 1.Ski-Jäger Brigade, Russian Front, Summer 1944

Fighting on the far northern sector of the Eastern Front, this junior officer from an army Ski-Jäger unit wears the army version of the Waffen-SS smock with the typical army 'splinter'-pattern camouflage effect. He wears the M43 field cap on the left flap of which is the Ski-Jager cap badge. The officer has an MP40 machine-pistol, and wears its attendant ammunition pouches on his waistbelt.

G2: SS-Schütze, 6. SS-Geb-Div. 'Nord', Lappland Front 1941

This Waffen-SS mountain troop private from the 'Nord' Division wears the second-pattern Waffen-SS smock, with foliage loops and skirt pockets, with the green summer pattern outermost. His headgear is the M43 cap with a camouflaged helmet cover added to achieve maximum concealment. Although it may appear odd, photographic evidence shows the occasional use of the helmet cover with the M43 cap. Camouflaged field caps were manufactured but were not as widely issued as other forms of headgear. In the field, the soldier often had to make do with whatever was available.

G3: Unteroffizier, Gebirgsjäger Regt. 137, Lappland front, Winter 1943

This ski-trooper sniper wears one of the myriad of different patterns of fur cap produced for personnel serving on the Eastern Front in the winter months. His smock is the second-pattern army type, with attached hood, worn with its white side outermost, and he has a pair of matching white overtrousers.

G4: Ski-Jäger sleeve patch
Machine-woven sleeve patch for Ski-Jäger units.

G5: Ski-Jäger cap badge
White metal Ski-Jäger badge worn on the left side of the field cap.

Late War, 1944-45
Anti-partisan operations, Balkans, 1943-44
H1: Jäger, Gebirgsjäger Regt. 98, Serbia, April 1943

This mountain troop machine-gunner on anti-partisan operations in the latter part of the war is heavily laden with rucksack and MG42 machine-gun. He wears the army version of the M43 tunic, with the subdued mouse grey insignia. The tool pouch for his MG42 is carried on the right of his waistbelt, and the weapon has been fitted with a drum magazine. His M42-pattern steel helmet has had a piece of camouflaged netting added.

H2: Unteroffizier, Gebirgsjäger Regt. 99, Yugoslavia, Autumn 1943

Few army units were as lavishly equipped with camouflaged clothing as were their Waffen-SS counterparts. The Zeltbahn of tent shelter quarter issued to each man could be worn in the form of a poncho, to give protection from rain and as a camouflage measure, as worn here.

H3: SS-Rottenführer, 7.SS-Frw-Geb-Div 'Prinz Eugen', Yugoslavia, Autumn 1943

This Waffen-SS mountain trooper from the 'Prinz Eugen' Division wears the camouflage helmet cover as well as the camouflage smock first pattern, which lacked the loops of later smocks. It was initially intended to be worn over the tunic, belt and equipment, slash openings on the smock giving access. Although photographs from the early stages of the war do show the smock worn like this, it soon became widespread practice to wear the belt and equipment over the smock, making access much easier. The smock has the predominantly brown, autumn, camouflage patterns outermost.

H4: Anti-partisan badge
Silver badge introduced in 1944. (See page 56).

7.SS-Frw-Geb-Div. 'Prinz Eugen'
I1: SS-Rottenführer, Perlycsac Peninsula,
Summer 1944

This Rottenführer of SS-Gebirgsjäger wears black ankle-boots with canvas gaiters into which his field grey wool trousers are tucked. His tunic is typical Waffen-SS style. It is all field grey, with five-button fastening, almost always seen worn with the top button undone and the collar pressed open. A black leather belt is worn, with the standard SS-pattern buckle, finished in a field grey colour, and pouches for the Kar 98k carbine. On his lower left sleeve is the divisional cuff-title 'Prinz Eugen'. A machine-embroidered sleeve eagle can be seen over the twin chevrons of his rank, in grey silk. His shoulder straps are black wool with light green piping. On his right collar the patch displays the Odal Rune emblem of the division, while the left patch shows a double strip of aluminium braid. His M43 field cap carries the Waffen-SS machine-woven cap insignia, but on the left flap is the machine-embroidered Edelweiss insignia of SS mountain units. He also wears a machine-embroidered Edelweiss patch on the right upper arm.

I2: SS-Hauptsturmführer, Yugoslavia, late 1943

This officer, from the same division, wears polished leather jackboots with grey-green breeches and an M36-style tunic with dark green collar and four pleated patch pockets. On his lower left sleeve is an officers' version of the divisional cuff-title, woven in aluminium thread. The shoulder straps he wears are in matt aluminium braid with two white metal rank pips and have light green intermediary underlay between the braid top and black wool base. His right collar patch shows the Odal Rune in aluminium embroidery, while the left shows three rank pips and two strips of aluminium braid, indicating his rank as SS-Hauptsturmführer. The Edelweiss patch on his right sleeve is identical to the other ranks' version. He wears the black leather waistbelt with officers'-pattern buckle and a black leather P08 holster. As headgear he wears the officers' version of the M43 cap with aluminium braid piping to the crown and with the eagle and deaths head insignia woven in aluminium thread.

I3: SS-Untersturmführer, SS-Panzer Abteilung 7, Drina Valley, Spring 1945

The 'Prinz Eugen' division also had an armoured detachment utilising mainly captured and obsolete enemy vehicles. This *SS-Untersturmführer* wears the standard Waffen-SS black Panzer clothing, with his trousers tucked into his ankle-boots. His collar patches bear the Odal Rune on the right and the three rank pips of his grade on the left. His sleeve eagle is woven in aluminium thread. His shoulder straps bear the piping intermediate underlay of armoured personnel, though the Edelweiss patch on his right sleeve still indicates his membership of a mountain unit. He wears an army-pattern black leather belt with double claw buckle (the circular SS officers' buckle was notorious for springing open). His headgear is the usual Waffen-SS officers' peaked cap with white piping (coloured piping on SS caps was extremely rare).

I4: SS-pattern Edelweiss sleeve patch

These were the same for officers and other ranks.

Ethnic Waffen-SS
J1: SS-Sturmbannführer, 13. W-Geb-Div. der 'Handschar', Northern Bosnia, Spring 1944

This German SS-Sturmbannführer attached to the 'Handschar' Division wears mountain-boots with his trousers tucked into canvas gaiters. He has the standard M36-style officers' tunic with hand-embroidered aluminium thread sleeve eagle. His collar patches show, on the right, the scimitar emblem of the division (but in its other ranks' form), machine-embroidered in silver-grey thread. It has, however, had officers' silver twist cord edging added. The left patch shows the four white metal pips of his rank. His shoulder straps have light green intermediary piping. On his left breast pocket, as a German national and full SS member, he wears the hand-embroidered SS runes patch. This was permitted for all full SS members operating with units not entitled to use the SS runes collar patch. The black leather belt with circular officers' buckle is worn. Head-dress consists of a burgundy fez with standard SS-pattern officers' cap insignia woven in aluminium wire.

J2: SS-Scharführer, 13.W-Geb-Div. der SS 'Handschar', Hungary, Autumn 1944

This SS-Scharführer from the same division as *I1* wears normal service dress comprising long field grey trousers, mountain-boots and puttees, worn with the M43 field blouse. On his left sleeve is a machine-woven sleeve eagle over a shield in the national colours.

The shoulder straps are made from black wool with aluminium braid edging. The right collar patch bears the scimitar/swastika emblem, while the left bears a single strip of aluminium braid with a single rank pip. The Edelweiss emblem is worn on the right sleeve. His black waistbelt carries the field grey painted SS buckle and the ammunition pouches for his machine pistol. His fez is the field service version in field grey felt. On his left breast pocket is the anti-partisan badge, which indicates that he has taken part in actions against Tito's partisans.

J3: SS-Hauptsturmführer, 21.W-Geb-Div. der SS 'Skanderbeg', Yugoslavia, May 1944

This is an SS-Hauptsturmführer from the 'Skanderbeg' division. He wears normal ankle-boots with canvas gaiters into which his trousers are tucked. His tunic is an officer quality version of the M43 field blouse with plain field grey collar. On his left sleeve is the divisional cuff-band woven in silver-grey silk thread on black. His sleeve eagle is the typical officers' style in hand-embroidered bullion wire, and is worn over a shield bearing the Albanian double-headed eagle on a red field.

The right hand collar patch shows the crested helmet insignia of the division. Though these were definitely manufactured, no photographic evidence of them being worn has yet surfaced. His left collar patch shows the three rank pips and two braid stripes of his grade. His headgear is the M43 cap. The deaths head insignia is worn to the front, with both the eagle and Edelweiss emblem to the side.

J4: SS cap insignia

Machine woven SS deaths head cap insignia which was worn on most forms of headgear including the fez.

Late War, 1944-45
K1: Unteroffizier, Gebirgsjäger Regt. 99, Hungary, December 1944

This Unteroffizier of Gebirgsjäger wears the M43-pattern service dress. The trousers in field grey wool are worn with canvas gaiters and ankle-boots. The M43-pattern tunic now has a plain field grey collar and four unpleated patch pockets with straight-cut flaps. The tunic has a six- rather than five-button fastening and both the collar patches and the breast eagle are woven in mouse-grey silk. The shoulder straps and tunic collar are trimmed in grey rather than aluminium braid. On the right sleeve is a machine-embroidered version of the Edelweiss patch, on field grey backing.

The normal black leather belt with field grey painted buckle is worn, as is the general issue M43 field cap. The NCO is a veteran of the Narvik battle as shown by the Narvik Shield worn on the upper left sleeve. Like many specialist troops, Gebirgsjäger often found themselves fighting as ordinary infantry, far from the mountain environments in which they excelled. This NCO, fighting somewhere on the Eastern Front against marauding Red Army tank formations, carries the excellent StG 44 assault rifle and Panzerfaust anti-tank projectile launcher.

K2:Kanonier, Gebirgs-Artillerie Regt. 111, Southern Germany, 1945

The final appearance of the mountain trooper in 1945 is reflected here. The jacket, of M44-pattern, is similar to the British battledress blouse, even having a distinctly brownish hue. It has two patch breast pockets and a distinct waistband. The eagle is now woven on a triangular backing – easier to manufacture and easier to sew to the tunic than the outline of the previous pattern. The shoulder straps have red piping, indicating that the soldier belongs to a mountain artillery unit. The steel helmet is worn with its camouflaged cover. Trousers of a similar brownish shade to the jacket are worn, with canvas gaiters and ankle-boots. Although the appearance of the mountain trooper had deteriorated somewhat, his weaponry has not: he carries the Gew.43 automatic rifle, and its distinctive pouches are carried on his standard black waist-belt.

K3: Hauptwachtmeister, Hochgebirgsgendarmerie, Southern Germany, 1945

The German police also maintained personnel trained for mountain service in the Alpine areas of the Reich. This mountain police NCO wears black leather mountain-boots and long field grey trousers bloused at the bottom, their ends tucked into his boots. The field grey worn by police units often had a more greenish hue than that used by the army, often referred to as 'police green'. His tunic has a contrasting mid-brown collar and cuffs, with four pleated patch pockets. The tunic has an eight-button fastening to the front and traditional orange Gendarmerie piping to the front, collar and cuffs. Gendarmerie-pattern collar patches and shoulder straps are worn, with a Gendarmerie-style orange thread embroidered arm eagle. He wears a *Bergmütze* with single-button fastening to the flap and orange piping to the crown. Insignia consists of a metal cockade over an aluminium Polizei-pattern cap eagle. A brown leather belt is worn, with a P38 pistol holster and aluminium Polizei-pattern buckle.

K4: Edelweiss arm patch

This is a wartime pattern machine embroidered patch on field grey backing.

Germany, 1944-45

L1: SS-Untersturmführer, 6.SS-Geb-Div. 'Nord', Saarland, Early 1945

Fighting in the defence of Germany in late 1944/early 1945, this officer is from the Nord Division. He wears the usual ankle-boots and canvas gaiters with field grey trousers, and an officers' version of the M36 field blouse. On the lower left sleeve is an officer-quality cuff-band woven in aluminium thread on black, with the legend 'Reinhard Heydrich'. His sleeve eagle is also woven in aluminium thread. As a German national he wears the standard SS runes collar patch on the right, and the three rank pips of the rank of SS-Untersturmführer on the left. Headgear is a late version of the officers' M43 cap, with its insignia woven in light grey thread on a field grey trapezoidal backing. The usual Edelweiss insignia is worn on the left side flap. An army-pattern belt with double claw buckle is worn, with a black leather holster for a P38 pistol.

L2: SS-Unterscharführer, 6.SS-Geb-Div. 'Nord', Thuringia, May 1945

This SS-Unterscharführer from the 'Nord' Division wears M44 service dress. Black leather ankle-boots and canvas gaiters are worn with the camouflaged-pattern trousers. On the lower left sleeve of his short battledress style blouse is the machine-woven cuff-band 'Michael Gaissmair' in grey thread on black. His sleeve eagle is also machine-woven in grey thread. The black woollen shoulder straps have grey silk NCO braid edging but, as was often the case in the latter stages of the war, no NCO braid has been fitted to the collar of his field blouse. He wears a machine-woven runic collar patch on his right collar and a single rank pip on his left collar patch. On his belt are the ammunition pouches for his superb StG 44 assault rifle. Headgear comprises the steel helmet with camouflaged cover.

L3: W-Rottenführer, 23. W-Geb-Div. der SS 'Kama', Croatia, late Autumn 1944

This Rottenführer is a Croat Moslem from the 'Kama' Division. He wears the standard field grey trousers with ankle-boots but instead of gaiters or puttees has rolled his socks down over the tops of the boots. The standard M43 field blouse is worn. The machine-woven arm eagle on the left sleeve is positioned over the twin chevrons of his rank. On the right upper sleeve is the Edelweiss arm patch. His shoulder straps are black wool with light green piping, and his left collar patch shows a double strip of aluminium braid indicating his rank. He wears a black leather belt with field grey painted buckle, leather Y-straps and triple pouches for his Kar 98k. Headgear is the field grey fez as worn by the 'Handschar' Division, though a field grey conical skullcap was also worn by this division.

L4: SS-pattern Edelweiss badge

This is the SS-pattern cap badge worn on the side of the *Bergmütze*.

Notes sur les planches en couleur

A1 Soldat Gebirgsjäger en uniforme de tous les jours. La tunique est en laine grise et les bandoulières sont bordées d'une ganse vert clair qui caractérise les troupes Jäger. *A2* Gebirgsjäger Hauptmann qui porte la tunique des officiers avec un col vert foncé. *A3* Général des troupes de montagne. On reconnaît son rang de général par la ganse rouge vif de sa tunique et l'écusson Eidelweiss des troupes de montagne.

B1 Un Jäger portant le Waffenrock ou uniforme de parade. *B2* est un Feldwebel. Il porte une ficelle de rang et un galon en aluminium sur le col, les poignets et les épaulettes, qui indique qu'il s'agit d'un sous-officier. *B3* Officier Waffenrock. Son état d'adjudant est indiqué par les aiguillettes en galon d'aluminium.

C1 Unteroffizier vers 1939 qui porte un uniforme normal. Le pantalon est toujours gris pierre car il n'a pas encore été remplacé par le modèle gris campagne. Sa ceinture a des sacs de munitions pour sa carabine Mauser Kar98k. *C2* représente le Général der Gebirgstruppe Deitl juste après la bataille de Narvik. Il porte la Croix des Chevaliers et le blason de Narvik obtenu pour cette bataille. *C3* est un Oberfeldwebel en Crète, 1942.

D1 Soldat des troupes de montagne vers 1940. Il porte le manteau standard des troupes. Ses chaussures de montagne ont une semelle double épaisseur à gros clous. Il porte le Kar98k standard. *D2* est un Sous-officier en uniforme de combat léger : tunique modèle M1936 avec galon de sous-officier sur le col et au bord des épaulette. *D3* Ce Sous-officier porte le smock des parachutistes par dessus ses vêtements normaux. Il porte un pistolet automatique MP38.

E1 Mitrailleur qui porte l'anorak côté gris dehors avec la 'queue' attachée entre les jambes. Il porte un pantalon gris campagne et des bandes molletières. *E2* Ce sous-officier de montagne porte l'uniforme tropical complet. *E3* Oberfeldwebel en Italie, 1944. Son uniforme est léger et le Bergmutze est souvent remplacé par la casquette M43.

F1 Oberfeldwebel qui porte la veste pare-vent standard des troupes, vêtement léger qui diminuait les effets du vent froid à haute altitude. *F2* Pour se protéger des terribles températures du front oriental, ce soldat de montagne porte des vêtements réversibles capitonnés, le côté blanc à l'extérieur. *F3* porte l'anorak réversible gris/blanc avec un sur-pantalon blanc et des chaussures de montagnes conçues pour le ski. Les moufles ont un doigt pour l'index (utilisé pour la gâchette).

G1 Officier junior d'une unité de Ski-Jäger dans le secteur extrême nord du front oriental, qui porte la version armée du smock Waffen-SS et une casquette de campagne M43. *G2* Soldat de montagne Waffen-SS, Division Nord. Il porte le second modèle de smock avec le motif vert 'd'été' à l'extérieur. *G3* Ce soldat sur skis porte l'un des nombreux modèles de casquettes de fourrure fabriquées pour le personnel du front oriental. Le soldat en campagne devait souvent se contenter de ce qui était disponible.

H1 Mitrailleur de troupes de montagne durant des opérations anti-partisanes vers la fin de la guerre. Son casque d'acier modèle M42 est recouvert d'un filet de camouflage, *H2* Ce soldat de montagne porte son Zeltbahn comme camouflage. *H3* Soldat de montagne Waffen-SS de la Division Prinz Eugen.

I1 Rottenführer des SS-Gebirgsjäger, Division Prinz Eugen. *I2* Officier de la même division qui porte une tunique M36 avec des bottes de cuir cirées et une culotte gris-vert. *I3* est un SS-Untersturmfuhrer en uniforme Waffen-SS noir Panzer.

J1 SS-Sturmbannführer rattaché à la Division Handschar, indiqué par l'emblème en forme de sceptre sur l'écusson du col droit. L'écusson des runes SS apparaît sur la poche de poitrine gauche. SS. *J2* SS-Scharführer de la même division en uniforme de service normal. Sur la poche de poitrine gauche on voit le badge anti-partisans qui indique sa participation à l'action contre les partisans de Tito. *J3* SS-Hauptsturmführer de la Division Skanderbegg, indiquée par l'écusson de son col droit.

K1 Unteroffizier en uniforme de service modèle M43. La tunique de modèle M43 a maintenant un col gris campagne et quatre poches appliquées sans plis, avec une patte droite. Il porte le bouclier Narvik et l'excellent fusil d'assaut StG44. *K2* Simple soldat en 1945. *K3* est un sous-officier de la police de montagne. La ganse orange indique qu'il s'agit d'un policier.

L1 SS-Untersturmführer, Division Nord, 1944/5. Comme il est de nationalité allemande, il porte l'écusson des runes SS sur la droite et ses trois ficelles de rang sur la gauche. *L2* SS-Unterscharführer, Division Nord en uniforme de service M44. *L3* Rottenfuhrer croate musulman pour la Division Kama. Les deux écussons de col sont noirs sans motif mais il porte l'écusson eidelweiss sur sa manche.

Farbtafeln

A1 Gefreiter der Gebirgsjäger im alltäglichen Dienstanzug. Der Rock ist aus grauem Wollstoff, an den Schulterstücken sieht man die hellgrauen Vorstöße der Jäger. *A2* Gebirgsjäger-Hauptmann im Offiziersrock mit dunkelgrünem Kragen. *A3* General der Gebirgstruppen. Er ist aufgrund der hellroten Vorstöße am Rock als General erkenntlich. Auf dem Tuchabzeichen auf dem Ärmel sieht man das Edelweiß der Gebirgstruppen.

B1 Jäger im Waffenrock der Ausgeuniform. *B2* Diese Abbildung zeigt einen Feldwebel. Er trägt den einzelnen Rangstern und Aluminiumlitze am Kragen, den Manschetten und den Schulterstücken, was ihn als Unteroffizier ausweist. *B3* Offizier im Waffenrock, sein Rang als Adjutant ist durch die Aluminiumlitzenabzeichen ersichtlich.

C1 Unteroffizier um 1939 im normalen Dienstanzug. Die Hosen sind noch steingrau, waren also noch nicht durch die feldgrauen ersetzt worden. An seiner Koppel sind Patronentaschen für seinen Mauser Kar98k Karabiner befestigt. *C2* Diese Abbildung zeigt den General der Gebirgstruppe Dietl unmittelbar nach der Schlacht von Narvik. Er trägt das Ritterkreuz und das Narvik-Abzeichen, das für Tapferkeit bei dieser Schlacht verliehen wurde. *C3* Diese Abbildung zeigt einen Oberfeldwebel beim Kampf auf Kreta 1942.

D1 Gefreiter der Gebirgstruppen um 1940. Er trägt den Mantel, der standardmäßig an die Mannschaften ausgegeben wurde. Seine Bergschuhe weisen schwer genagelte Sohlen doppelter Stärke auf. Er hat das übliche Kar98k bei sich. *D2* Diese Abbildung zeigt einen Unteroffizier im leichten Kampfanzug: ein Rock des Modells M1936 mit Unteroffizierslitze am Kragen und am Rand der Schulterstücke. *D3* Dieser Unteroffizier trägt den Fallschirmspringeranzug der Luftwaffe über seiner normalen Kleidung. Er hat eine Maschinenpistole MP38 bei sich.

E1 Maschinengewehrschütze im Anorak mit der grauen Seite nach außen. Das "Schoßband" ist zwischen den Beinen befestigt. Er trägt feldgraue Hosen und Wickelgamaschen. *E2* Dieser Unteroffizier der Gebirgsjäger ist in kompletter Tropenausstattung. *E3* Feldwebel in Italien, 1944. Seine Uniform ist aus leichtem Stoff, und die Bergmütze wurde weitgehend durch die Feldmütze M43 ersetzt.

F1 Oberfeldwebel in der standardmäßigen Windjacke der Gebirgstruppen. Dabei handelte es sich im eine leichte Jacke, die vor dem schneidenden Wind in den höheren Lagen schützen sollte. *F2* Zum Schutz vor den eiskalten Temperaturen an der Ostfront trägt dieser Gebirgsjäger warm gefütterte, umkehrbare Bekleidung, mit der weißen Seite nach außen. *F3* Diese Figur trägt den umkehrbaren Anorak mit einer grauen und einer weißen Seite mit weißen Überhosen und Bergschuhen, die zum Skifahren gedacht waren. Die Fausthandschuhe haben einen Finger für den Schußfinger.

G1 SS-Untersturmführer, Nord Division, 1944/45. Als Deutscher trägt er das SS-Abzeichen am Kragen auf der rechten Seite und seine drei Rangsterne auf der linken. *G2* SS-Unterscharführer, Nord Division, im Dienstanzug M44. *G3* Ein kroatischer, moslemischer Rottenführer der Kama Division. Beide Kragenspiegel sind schwarz ohne Motiv, auch trägt das Edelweiß-Abzeichen am Arm.

H1 Maschinengewehrschütze der Gebirgstruppe bei Partisanenjägermaßnahmen in der letzten Kriegsphase.Trommelmagazin ausgerüstet ist. Sein Stahlhelm des Modells M42 hat ein Tarnnetz. *H2* Dieser Gebirgssoldat macht sich seine Zeltbahn als Tarnung zunutze. *H3* Gebirgssoldat der Waffen-SS von der Prinz Eugen Division.

I1 Rottenführer der SS-Gebirgsjäger, Prinz Eugen Division. *I2* Offizier der gleichen Division im Waffenrock des Musters M36 mit gewichsten Lederstiefeln und graugrünen Reithosen. *I3* Diese Abbildung zeigt einen SS-Untersturmführer in der schwarzen Panzerkleidung der Waffen-SS.

J1 SS-Sturmbannführer bei der Handschar-Division, ersichtlich durch das Krummsäbel-Emblem auf dem rechten Kragenspiegel. Das SS-Abzeichen taucht auf der linken Brusttasche auf. *J2* SS-Scharführer von der gleichen Division im normalen Dienstanzug. Auf seiner linken Brusttasche sieht man das Partisanenkämpfer-Abzeichen, das belegt, daß er an Maßnahmen gegen Titos Partisanen teilnahm. *J3* SS-Hauptsturmführer von der Skanderbeg-Division, was durch den rechten Kragenspiegel ersichtlich ist.

K1 Unteroffizier im Dienstanzug des Modells M43. Der Rock der Machart M43 weist jetzt einen einfarbigen, feldgrauen Kragen auf sowie vier aufgesetzte Taschen ohne Quetschfalte mit gerade geschnittenen Taschenklappen. *K2* Einfacher Soldat 1945.Er trägt ein Automatikgewehr Gew 43 und Patronentaschen bei sich.*K3* Hier handelt es sich um einen Unteroffizier der Gebirgspolizei. Die orangefarbenen Vorstöße machen ihn als Polizisten erkenntlich.

L1 Rangniedriger Offizier einer Skijäger-Einheit der Armee beim Gefecht im nördlichsten Sektor der Ostfront. Er trägt die Armeeversion des Anzugs der Waffen-SS und die Feldmütze M43. *L2* Gebirgstruppe der Waffen-SS, Nord Division. Er trägt den Kittel des zweiten Musters mit dem grünen "Sommer"-Muster nach außen. *L3* Dieser Skisoldat trägt eine der zahlreichen Modelle von Pelzmützen, die für die Mannschaften an der Ostfront bereitgestellt wurden.